Pega How-to Guide

Exporting Data to Excel
(How-to Version)

© Debunkum Beaver 2020. All Rights Reserved.
https://www.DebunkumBeaver.com

Copyright Notice

No part of this publication may be reproduced,
stored in a retrieval system, or transmitted in any form or
by any means, electronic, mechanical, photocopying, recording,
scanning, or otherwise, without the prior written
consent of the author.

This publication is meant for personal use,
as a reference for pursuing the Pega CLSA Certification.
The content shall not be used for any commercial purposes, including but not
limited to using this publication as a courseware / training aid without
the prior written consent of the author. By purchasing this
publication, you own the physical media (books, ebooks),
not its knowledge nor the content.

In support of academic knowledge sharing,
an abridged version of the book is published at the author's site:
https://www.DebunkumBeaver.com
You may reference the information available there, as long as a statement is
included and a link back to the blog version of the publication. You may quote or
reference any information in this book, but you must state the source of the
information, such as the name of the book and author.
Please check with the author if you
have any special requests.

Pega®, the Pega Logo are trademarks of Pegasystems Inc.
VirtualBox is a trademark of Oracle, registered in various countries.
All other companies, products, or service names may be trademarks or service
marks of others and are the property of their respective owners.

References made to the respective trademarks within
this publication are meant for clarification and discussion purposes,
it does not constitute or imply any acknowledgement,
acceptance or endorsement of this publication.

Copyright © DebunkumBeaver.com 2020
Published By Golden AT
ISBN: 9789811703119

Disclaimer

The content within the publication is based solely on the
author's personal knowledge and experiences, and it does not represent any
other entities' views, either directly, or implied.

Readers' should view this publication as another point of view,
use it as a reference and sought their own conclusion.

Although the author and publisher
have made every effort to ensure that the
information in this book was correct at time of print,
the author and publisher do not assume and hereby disclaim any
liability to any party for any loss, damage, or disruption
caused by errors or omissions, whether such
errors or omissions result from
negligence, accident, or any
other causes.

The information in this book
is meant to supplement, not replace Pega Academy trainings.
Readers should ensure that they have completed the relevant Pega courses,
and to consult Pega Academy on matters related
to their trainings or certifications.

This is a non-official guide, and it is
created as a form of knowledge sharing, and presented as it is
without any warranties. Usage is entirely
at the reader's own risk.

By reading and using information in this
book, you signified your acceptance of these and assume all
responsibilities for its usage.

Dedication & Acknowledgements

First of all, I think we all need to thank
Alan Trefler, without him, there would not be the Pega
we are seeing today. It is also him, who kept Pega as a free company,
which was evident in the Reuters article on 'rather
eat sand than sell to other companies'.
Hopefully, Pega will continue
to be independent.

Special thanks to my dear wife
for the support provided for me to achieve
the CLSA certification, as well as the sacrificed family time
and encouragement she had provided me with to leverage on my academic
knowledge to contribute back to the community through this book.
Not to forget my boy, who volunteered to create a logo for
Debunkum Beaver, at the same time,
being my proof reader!

There were multiple great
SSAs/LSAs along my journey, who had
explained many important Pega concepts and guided
me in the past years. Their untiring explanations
and demonstrations are
greatly appreciated.

This book is a
dedication to all those who
would like to embark on the Pega Learning Journey.
With this, you now have one more
reliable resource.

Contents

COPYRIGHT NOTICE 2
DISCLAIMER 3
DEDICATION & ACKNOWLEDGEMENTS 4
CONTENTS 5
WHO IS THIS BOOK FOR? 9
PREFACE 10

    WHY CREATE A PEGA HOW-TO GUIDE? 10
    HOW SHOULD I CATEGORISE THE PEGA HOW-TO GUIDE? 14
    HOW SHOULD I ORGANISE EACH HOW-TO GUIDE? 17

VERSIONS OF PEGA HOW-TO GUIDE 19

    WHICH VERSION SHOULD I GET? 20
        Online Version *20*
        How-to Version *20*
        Master Beaver Version *20*

AUTHOR'S PROFILE 22
WHY NOT DO THIS AT PEGA COMMUNITY? 23

    LIMITED AND LACK OF CONTROL 23
    LACK OF DETAILS 23
    I WANT TO TEACH AND HAVE STUDENTS WHO WANT TO LEARN 24

INTRODUCTION 25

    PURPOSE OF THIS "EXPORTING DATA TO EXCEL" PEGA HOW-TO GUIDE 25

APPROACH USED FOR THIS GUIDE 27
PART 1: COMPLETING THE GROUNDWORK 29
CREATE A NEW APPLICATION 31
CREATE SAMPLE TEST USER 39

    CREATING NEW USERS FOR THE APPLICATION 39
        Profile Tab *41*
        History tab *41*

  Work Tab 42
  Security tab 42
  Enable Diagnostic Features 44
  Testing the DBeaver User 45
 GRANT EXISTING USER WITH ACCESS TO THE NEW APPLICATION 46

CREATING CASE TYPE, FLOW & SECTION 49

MODIFYING THE UI TO LIST DATA 59

 REUSING THE EXISTING REPORT DEFINITION (RD) 59
 MODIFYING THE "LISTUSERS" SECTION 61
 TESTING THE LISTING 64

PART 2: EXPORTING DATA TO EXCEL 67

INTRODUCING METHOD 1: USING PREDEFINED EXCEL TEMPLATE 69

METHOD 1: CREATING EXCEL FILE TEMPLATE 71

 UPLOAD THE TEMPLATE AS A BINARY FILE 71

METHOD 1: ADDING A BUTTON IN SECTION 75

METHOD 1: CREATING THE SCRIPT 77

 ADDING THE JS INTO A HARNESS 80

METHOD 1: CREATING THE ACTIVITY 83

TESTING METHOD 1 87

INTRODUCING METHOD 2: WITHOUT ANY NEW RULES 89

METHOD 2: CALLING THE SCRIPT FUNCTION 91

METHOD 2: INCLUDING THE REQUIRED SCRIPT 93

TESTING METHOD 2 95

SUMMARY 97

PART 3: MASTER BEAVER DISCUSSION 99

ADDING A NEW REPORTING FIELD 101

 MODIFY THE REPORT DEFINITION 101
  Fixing the Date Format for the UI Display 101
 METHOD 1 GENERATION WITH NEW COLUMN 102
 METHOD 2 GENERATION WITH NEW COLUMN 102
 UPDATING EXCEL TEMPLATE FOR METHOD 1 102

CHANGING METHOD 1 TO USE DATAPAGE 103

 UPDATE DOEXCELEXPORT TO USE DATAPAGE 104

RUNNING WITH NEW D_GETLISTOFOPERATORS 104
FIXING THE DATE TIME FORMAT 104
   Update the New Field in the Template *104*
   Upload the New Template *105*
   Modify the Datapage *105*
   Update the DoChangeListOfOperatorResponse DT *105*
   Testing the Formatted Date Time of Method 1 .... *106*

CONCLUSION **107**

INTRODUCING PEGA SNIPPETS SERIES **109**
   WHAT IS THE MAIN DIFFERENCE BETWEEN SNIPPETS AND HOW-TO SERIES?............. 109
   HOW IS PEGA SNIPPETS DISTRIBUTED AND THE PRICE? 110

OTHER BOOKS IN THE COLLECTIONS **113**

Who Is This Book For?

This Guide: **Debunkum Beaver Pega How-to Guide** is a series for everyone, people who are new to Pega as well as those who are experienced in Pega.

The prerequisite is just to have some basic understanding of Pega, preferably to have at least completed the Pega CSA training.

Being certified in Pega is not required, but a keen desire to learn Pega is a must!

Preface

Thanks for purchasing Debunkum Beaver Pega How-to Guide! In order to fully maximise the book, it is important to understand the purposes and positioning of this How-to series.

Why Create a Pega How-to Guide?

Strictly speaking, information on Pega "how-to" can be found in Pega Community, Pega Academy, as well as throughout the Internet.

Even if the information is not readily available, all that is needed is simply to create a new Pega Community post; and somehow, after some time, there would be people from the community, Pega GCS or even Pega Engineering, jumping in to provide the answer, so isn't such a how-to guide unnecessary?

Well, technically, you could argue it in that way. However, in any engagement, one of the most challenging things is "deadline". Often, a go-live date would be defined well before requirement specification is signed off.

Therefore, there is basically no time to search for information, wait for replies, or learn and explore how to implement certain features/requirements in an actual project scenario, at the time when it is required.

Apart from that, the replies are often not an end-to-end, step-by-step guide, complete with screenshots and do not include validation and testing steps. Thus, it would require prior Pega knowledge and additional effort to clarify, test and finally implement it.

To add on to the challenges, the profile of the team members often creates another dimension of issues. This problem has 2 extremities:

1) **New Users of Pega:** Those who are totally new to Pega
2) **Senior and Experienced Pega SSA/LSA:** Those who have many years of experiences, some even spanned across Pega V5.x and V6.x

For New Users of Pega, they do not know how to implement a lot of things in Pega, thus a lot of handholding and samples are required to guide them along and get them to be efficient.

There is technically not much issues with them, just the need to provide them with some relevant examples, or even implement one instance of the solution, explain to them how it works, and they would be able to get started and replicate the implementation across other parts of the application.

The downside is that a lot of time is required to create relevant samples and also to help them in debugging issues that may occur.

On the other hand, Senior and Experienced Pega SSAs/LSAs, although are self-starters and able to start implementation without much guidance, they introduced another kind of problem – their solutions to all problems are often "activities" and "agents"!!!

Any other issues that cropped up along the way, would often be yet another activity, custom Java codes or some HTML, JavaScripts; the worst that I have seen, was creating multiple Boolean variables to cater for various flows and decisions throughout the whole application for handle difference scenario and business changes!!!

With all those Boolean variables, in order to understand the whole logic (and ensure it is correct), you need to kept track of all the Boolean variables that are set/unset throughout all the activities, data transforms, flows, UIs, button clicked, etc.! Isn't that a BIG pain? How could the application ever be reliable?

Technically, they can implement the required features, but whatever they had touched, can no longer be easily modified by another SSA/LSA without the corresponding number of years of experience, not to mention about the underlying performance and maintenance issues that were introduced!

In view of all these challenges, Debunkum Beaver has decided to embark on this path: A How-to Guide for Pega.

For New Users of Pega, this series provide a step-by-step guide to implement any given feature; for Senior and Experienced Pega SSAs/LSAs, this guide shows the best practices and a standardised way of implementing the intended features, leveraging on the newer Pega capabilities to simplify the implementation, as much as possible.

With the Debunkum Beaver Pega How-to Guide series, you would have an arsenal of tools at your disposal. Whenever there is a new project, or a new feature required, all you have to do is just to pull out one of these guides. Cool right?

Can you visualise a situation, where all similar features have the same way of implementation, with the same sequence of steps and number of rules; and anyone who looked at the rules knew exactly how and why each rule was implemented as such; any deviations and bugs that were introduced due to carelessness would simply stand out by itself, easily identifiable and easy to fix, wouldn't this be a wonderful Pega World?

Well, that is the core objective of the **Debunkum Beaver Pega How-to Guide** series!

With the direction set, the next question is: "How Should I Categorise the Pega How-to Guide?"

How Should I Categorise the Pega How-to Guide?

Given that there are so many features, I couldn't just write <u>ONE book</u>, it would take ages, and by then, a new Pega version would be released!

Of course, I could potentially do a high-level grouping, e.g. *Pega Integration, Pega Reporting, Pega Case Management*, etc...

But there is one big problem...

Take *Pega Integration* as an example, there are so many types of integrations: SOAP, REST, OAuth2, etc. Does that mean that I should write all the integrations before publishing the *"Pega Integration"* book?

That would also take a long time, increase the overall price of the book and force readers to pay for things they do not need or are not interested in; worst, it would just end up as another version of Pega help file.

On top of that, if one of the integration methods changed, do I need to update the whole book as a new version?

Apart from the above issues, you may have realised another problem: I have not mentioned about another dimension of Integration: *Service Packages* vs *Service Connectors*!

So, should I have a book on *Pega Integration Service Connectors* and another on *Pega Integration Service Packages*? But I cannot separate them because I need to use the *Service Connectors* to invoke the *Service Packages* to test!

As you can see, things just get more and more messy...

I shared my problem with my boy, and asked him what books he enjoyed the most, and this is what he showed me - His private Mr Men Collection!

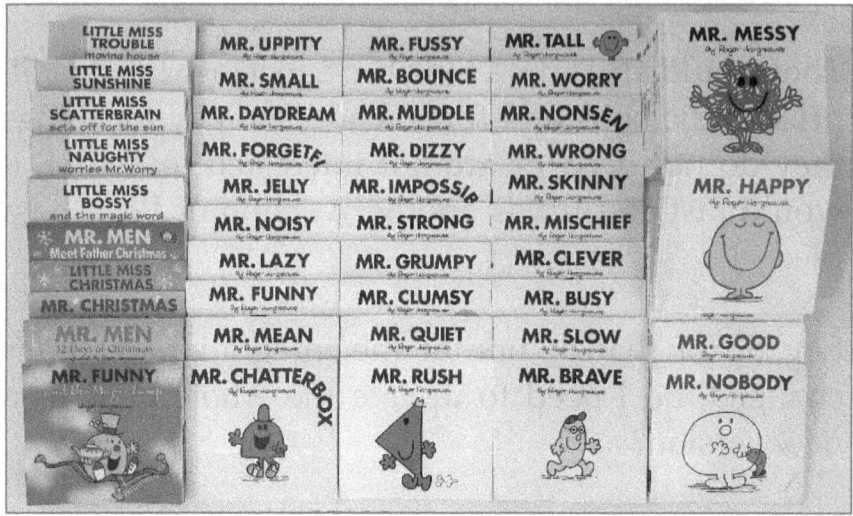

Figure 1: Mr Men Collection

He went on to explain how much he enjoyed the book. Although each single book is short, it is concise, and he can easily look for any Mr Men he wants; at the same time, priding himself as Mr Happy...

Well, although I feel Mr Messy is a better match for him, I agree on his concept: small little book that is concise, and easy to be used as a reference!

Yes! That is exactly how the Debunkum Beaver Pega How-to Guide would be released!

The next question is: How should I organise each Pega How-to Guide, so that it would achieve the core objective?

How Should I Organise Each How-to Guide?

I want to have a how-to guide suitable for both beginners and experts, one that could be used as a quick reference, yet without the unnecessary theories and documentation.

Yes, this is really a tall order, but anything less than that would not serve the purpose and would just end up being another Pega Community post or simply an excerpt of the Pega help file!

It must be able to provide something like a 2-mins run-through to illustrate the purpose and concept, like the typical "Hello World!" of programming, yet able to be expanded further into more useful stuff!

So here, Debunkum Beaver Pega How-to Guide is born! It sets out to achieve the above by applying the following:

1) Quick explanation of the purpose of the feature
2) A quick implementation using the typical "Hello World" style, demonstrating the feature in the simplest form
3) Expansion of the example using various scenario and extension of the feature to cover related areas

In order to provide a quick explanation and make understanding of Pega concepts a breeze, at times, I might "state" that a given Pega feature is equivalent to something that is more commonly understood, followed by a series of scenario that further extend its capabilities and enable users to slowly appreciate the differences.

For example, I might start by stating: "Think of Pega Data classes as Database tables...", and then proceeded with some scenario on how to use Pega Data Classes to add, update and delete records, followed by other interesting features, that would extend it capability and moved beyond just database tables.

So, take note of this unique approach in the guide.

Versions of Pega How-To Guide

In order to launch the book fast and to contribute to the overall Pega community knowledge, the Pega How-to Guide will be released in 3 versions:
1) **Online Version:** This is a free version, published at DebunkumBeaver.com. Basically, selected chapters are published and contained all the information required to implement the intended feature. The details and quality of the instructions would often exceed those that are freely available on the Internet.
2) **How-to Version**: This version contains all the details steps, including complete screenshots on how to implement the intended feature. You can be sure that it would DEFINITELY work, because I had simplified the steps, and redo it from scratch. Anything lesser than that would not meet the earlier set out objectives, agree?
3) **Master Beaver Version**: This version contains everything of the How-to Version, with the inclusion of analysis and reasons for doing the

given steps, as well as special scenario and limitations of the feature.

Note:
Debunkum Beaver Pega How-to Guide is using Pega 7.4.

Which Version Should I Get?

Online Version

If you are an experienced Pega architect and just need some pointers and have the time to investigate and try out the details, this version suits your needs.

By comparing this version with the How-to version, You will be able to better appreciate my purpose of creating the Pega How-to Guide series, as well as its value.

How-to Version

This version is for people who just want to implement the feature in the quickest possible way. This version takes the readers through a step-by-step procedure, with complete screenshots, thus suitable for new users of Pega, who wants to learn how to implement various features in Pega.

Master Beaver Version

If you are looking for more in-depth discussion, understand how and why the given feature was done in that way. This version is for you.

Most importantly, if you are considering taking Pega CLSA certification, it is always better to get the Master Beaver Version.

Author's Profile

The author is a Pega CLSA, certified in the new Pega CLSA Path (7.3/7.4). Academically, he has a master's degree and has experiences in teaching undergraduates pursuing master's and bachelor's degrees in World renowned universities.

Combining the above with his over 20 years of IT experiences in various MNCs, the author decided to write this series of Pega How-to Guide to help aspiring system architects to implement Pega in a faster, cleaner, and more efficient way.

Why Not Do This At Pega Community?

This is an interesting option that I had considered before. However, there are a few stoppers:

Limited and Lack of Control
I hate the feeling of being restricted. I have many ideas, plans and ways of doing things, but when there are people or situations that restrict or delay me, I get very pissed off.

Lack of Details
Pega Community is good but often, the replies are just one-liner, link to other articles, and a bunch of description and steps, which would not help if you do not have good Pega knowledge in the first place. Interestingly, if you had that, you would not need to go there to search for answers in the first place!

Please note that I am not saying that Pega Community does not provide good information or solutions, it is just that it was not meant to teach and guide you like what you were taught in your undergraduate studies.

I Want To Teach and Have Students Who Want to Learn

The platform today, and possibly many years into the future, focuses on the technicality of how to do a task, not about the purpose, or the thought process that led to the solution, which are crucial skills you will want to acquire if you want to be a good architect.

I needed a platform to allow me to do that, but in Pega Community, people have a stronger tendency to listen only to those 'renowned professional', who sometimes went down the 'too technical' path.

Therefore, there is basically no avenue that I could share the detailed and vast knowledge that I have.

Since I am an author, have the academic background, as well as a Pega CLSA, it makes perfect sense for me to do it through publication, thus, the birth of this book.

I want to teach, and if you want to learn, then welcome to the mind-blowing world of Debunkum Beaver!

Introduction

In Pega, we are often required to provide some search functionalities for users, such as listing records matching some given search criteria.

This is simple and OOTB. However, sometimes, the users might require us to provide a functionality to export the search results into Excel.

This would require some configurations, which are also quite simple.

Purpose of this "Exporting Data to Excel" Pega How-to Guide

The purpose of this "Exporting Data to Excel" Pega How-to Guide is to provide you with 2 methods of exporting the required data to Excel.

The 1st method, which is quite old, still works. However, it requires you to configure quite a few tasks. Any changes would require updating the template; worst, it has some limitations that will be explained in the Master Beaver Version.

The 1st method is quite freely available on the Internet, although I have come across several comments stating that it did not work.

To be fair to those bloggers, the steps are logical. The difficulties were likely because it was documented from an existing application (which may have some settings already in place that were not highlighted). It could also be that the bloggers had made assumptions on the knowledge of the readers.

Thus, the need for the "***Debunkum Beaver Pega How-to Guide***" approach!

As for the 2nd method, it is much simpler, to the extent that you might proclaim: "Why didn't anyone tell me about this method?!!"

Approach Used for This Guide

To keep things simple, we are not going to create any Datapages or Report Definitions, we will reuse those that are already in the system, so as to focus strictly on the exporting of the data to excel.

The following are the tasks that I will be performing:
1) Setup the Groundwork
   - Create an application
   - Create a Case Type with only 1 step, displaying the data
2) Add 2 buttons on the page to export the data to Excel, the 1st button will export using the 1st method, while the 2nd button will export using the 2nd method
3) Implement both the methods.

Part 1: Completing the Groundwork

Create A New Application

We shall create everything from scratch, including the creation of the application. By doing it this way, new users of Pega would be able to follow all the instructions; at the same time, we will end up with a "knowledge pack", that is standalone, and easier to understand and share among the team.

Note:
If you are an experience Pega user, you can just skip the groundwork and jump straight to adding the rules for the 2 methods.

Login as a user who has the rights to create application, e.g. `administrator@pega.com` (default pwd is `install`).

Click on the following menu item: *"Application:XXX > New Application"*

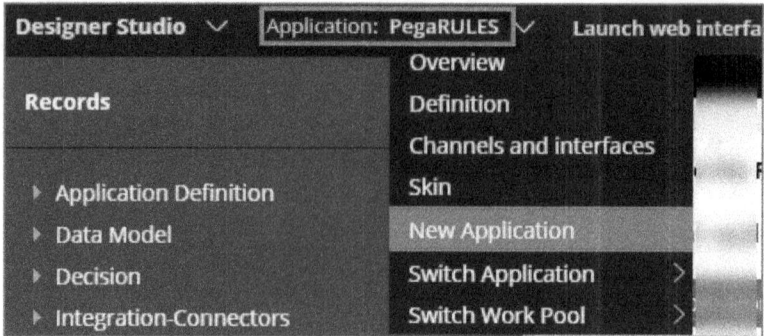

Figure 2: Creating a New Application

Note:
Don't worry about the "PegaRULES" on the right side of the "Application:" as shown in the diagram. By default, that shows the application that you are currently in, which does not really matter when you are just creating a new application.

In the form that opens, click on the "*Custom*" as shown below:

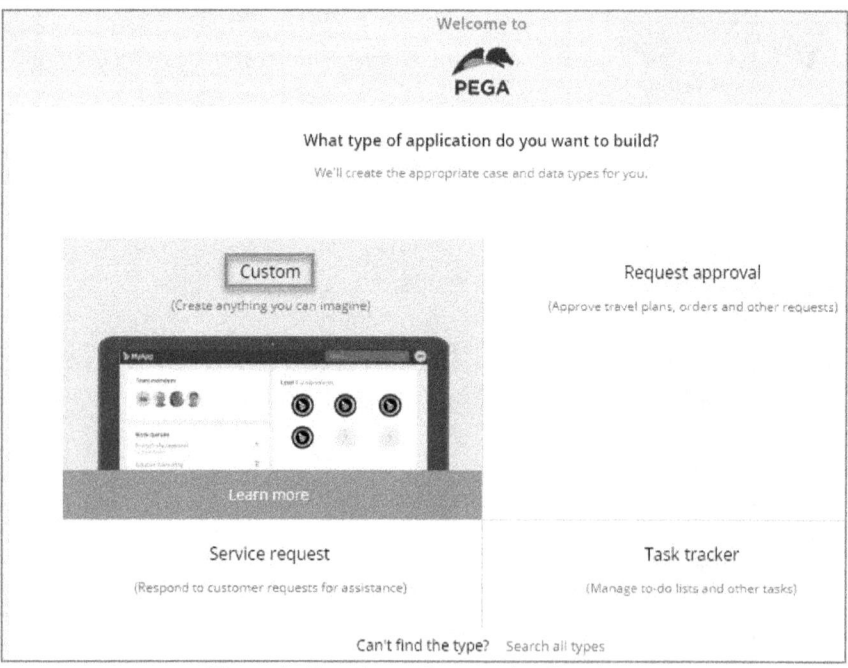

Figure 3: Creating a Custom Application

Click on the "*Use this application type*" to proceed.

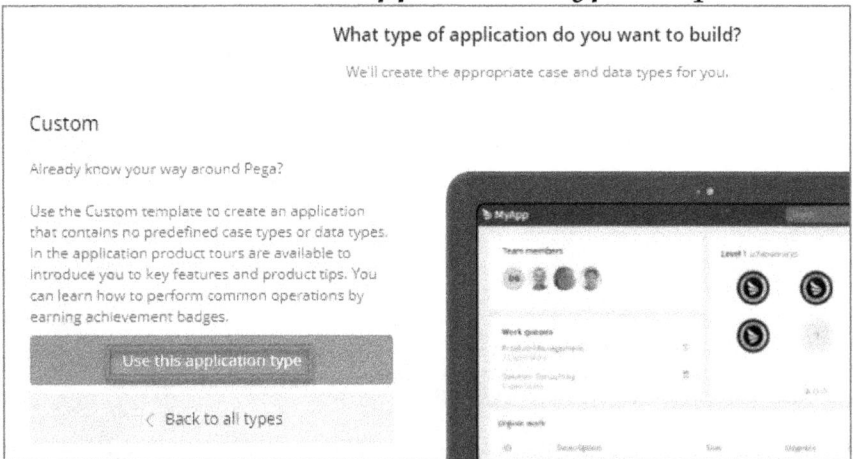

Figure 4: Confirming the Application Type

For the primary device, select "*Responsive*" as shown below:

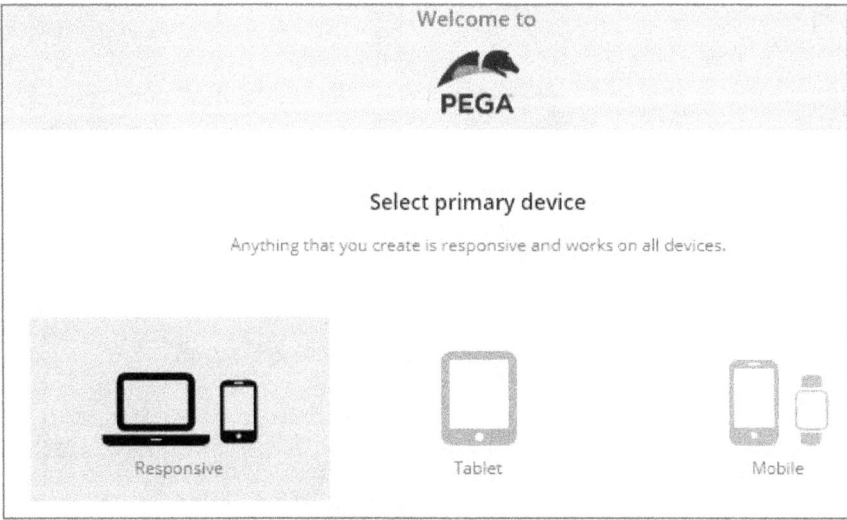

Figure 5: Selecting Responsive as the Primary Device

For the colour scheme, just choose the "*Default*".

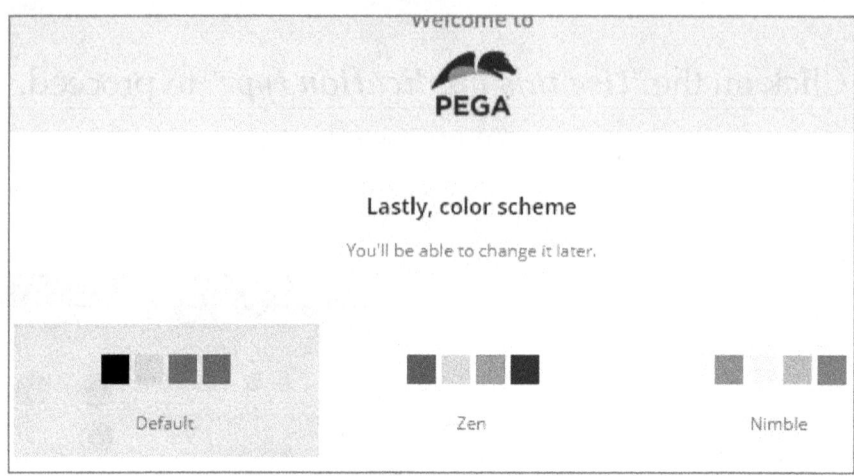

Figure 6: Selecting the Default Colour Scheme

Name your application as: "*ExpXLS*", followed by clicking on the "*Advanced configuration*" link.

 Note:
The following diagram shows the "ExpXLS" application as an example, you should name it according to your intended name.

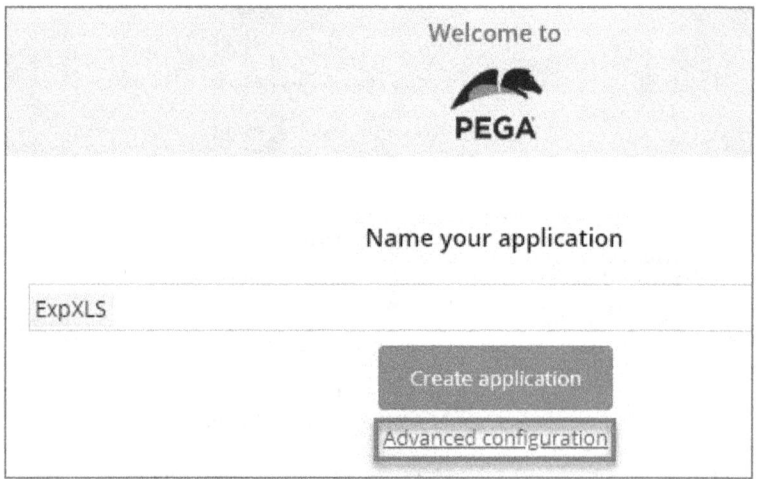

Figure 7: Sample of Application Name Screen for ExpXLS Application

In the "*Advanced configuration*" dialog shown below, ensure the following:
- Application structure: *Implementation*
- Application id: *ExpXLS*
- Organization name: *DB*
- Application: *ExpXLS*

The following is an example of the configuration.

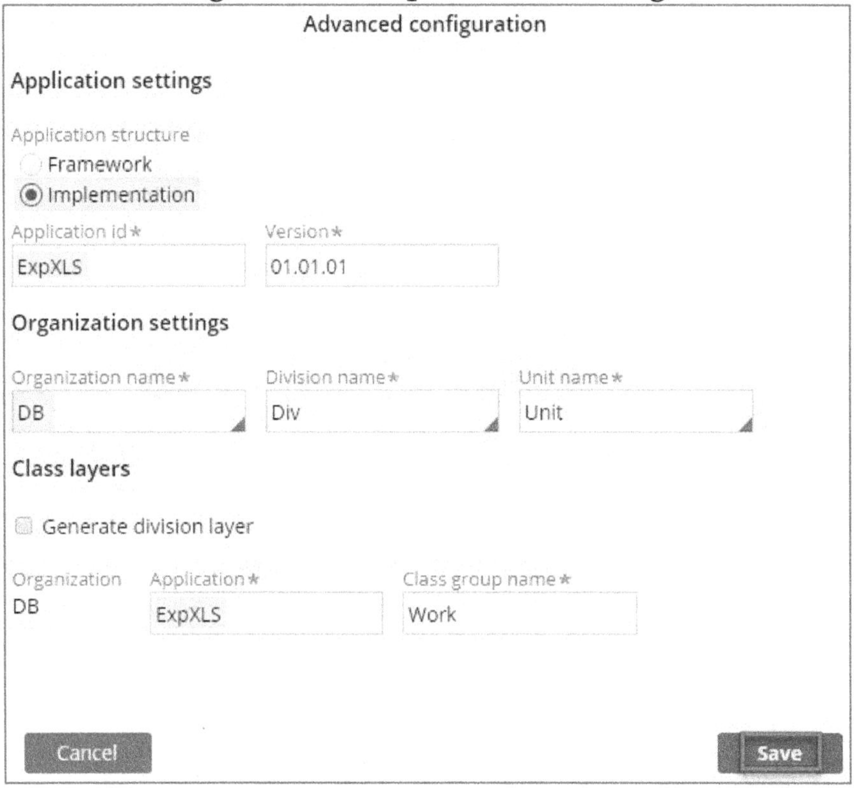

Figure 8: Sample of Advanced Configuration for ExpXLS Application

Click on the Save button to continue.

> **Note:**
> *If you are a new user of Pega, please follow exactly as above to avoid any problems. The details of these settings are out of the scope of this book.*

You will now be brought back to the "*Name your application*" page, as shown below. Click on the "*Create application*" to create it.

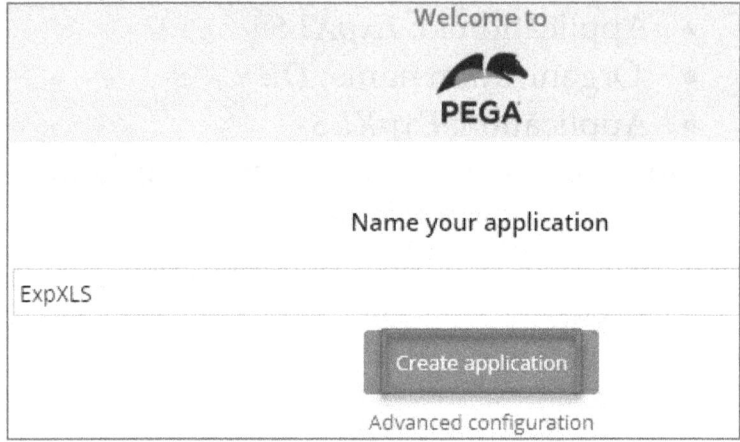

Figure 9: Example of Creating the ExpXLS Application

Once your application had been created, you will see the following confirmation:

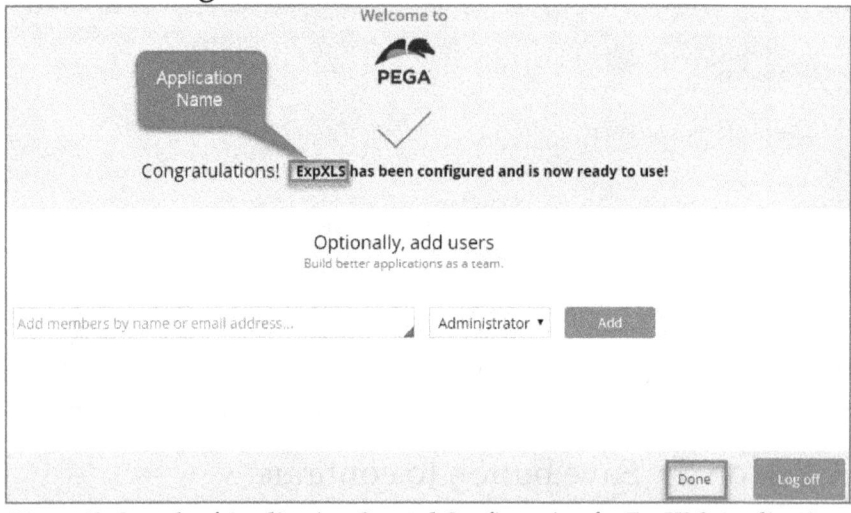

Figure 10: Sample of Application Created Confirmation for ExpXLS Application

At this point, you could create new users by entering the name or email address. However, we shall not do it this way as it had assumed that many settings are already configured in the existing system, such as existing users, email server settings, etc.

Therefore, let us just click on the "*Done*" button to close this dialog box.

Note:
In earlier versions of Pega, sample users are created, which is no longer the case in Pega 7.4.

To validate that your application is created, click on the Records Explorer (marked as 1), in the opened menu, under the "*Application Definition*", click the "*Application*" (marked as 2). You will now be able to see your newly created application on the right as shown below.

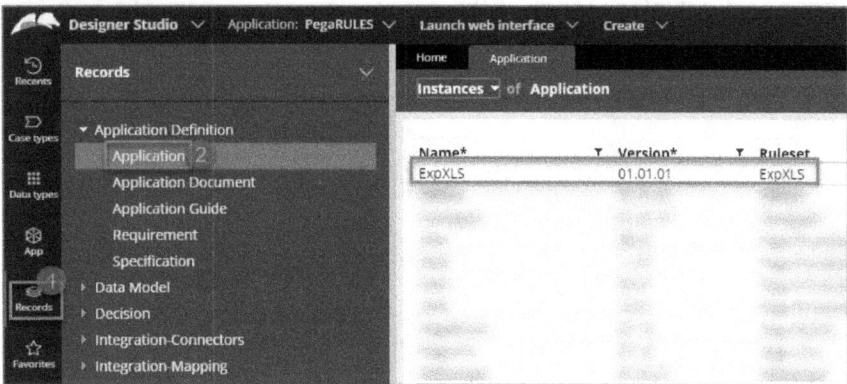

Figure 11: Example of Validating that ExpXLS Application Is Created

Apart from the application, you should also validate that your Access Groups are also created.

In the Records Explorer, under Security, click the "*Access Group*" menu item as shown below:

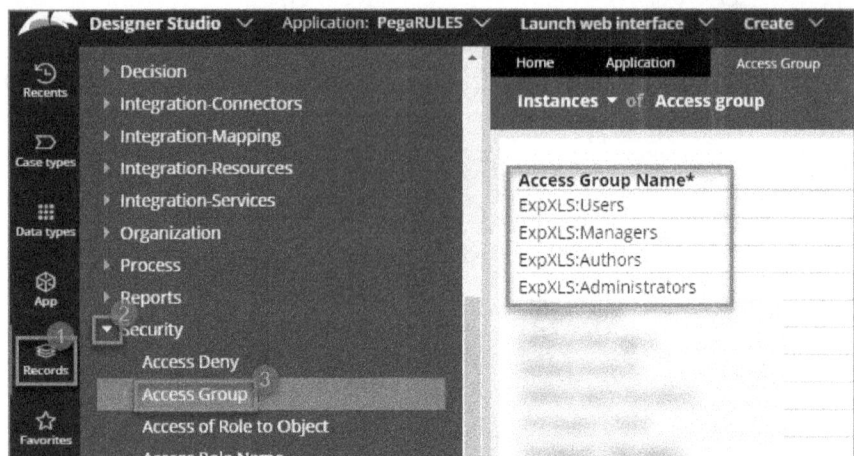

Figure 12: Example of Validating that ExpXLS Access Groups Are Created

You should see 4 Access Groups related to your created application. The above is an example for the "*ExpXLS*" application.

Create Sample Test User

Next, we shall create a sample test user to facilitate demonstration and testing. The user will be named "*DBeaver*", who is the administrator of the application.

For simplicity, we will also use the same user in other Pega How-to Guides. Therefore, if you had already created this user, you do not need to create it again.

However, you will still need to assign them with access to the new access group for your new application. Both instructions are shown below, please follow the steps in the relevant section.

Creating New Users for The Application
To create new users, follow these steps:
1) Click on Records Explorer
2) Look for "*Organization*" and click its arrow on the left to expand it
3) Right-click on the "*Operator ID*"
4) On the context menu that pops up, click on the "*Create*"

The following diagram illustrates the steps:

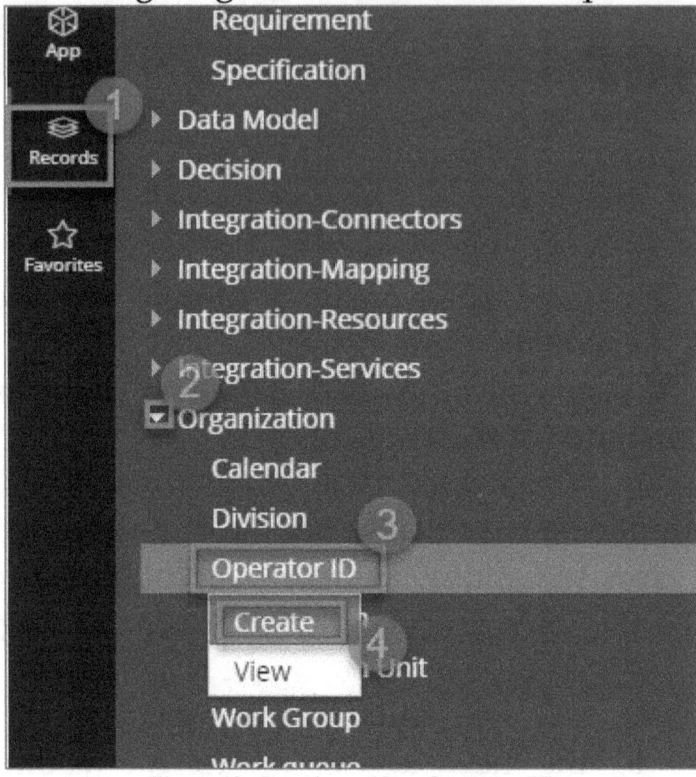

Figure 13: Creating a New Operator ID

On the create form, enter "*DBeaver*" for both the fields shown below, followed by clicking the "*Create and open*" button:

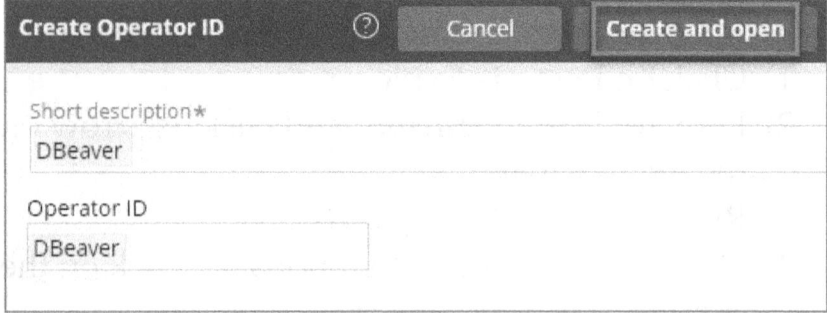

Figure 14: Creating Operator ID

With the DBeaver Operator ID opened, under the "*Profile*" tab, set the access group as "*ExpXLS:Administrators*".

Profile Tab

The following screen shows a sample of the "*Profile*" tab.

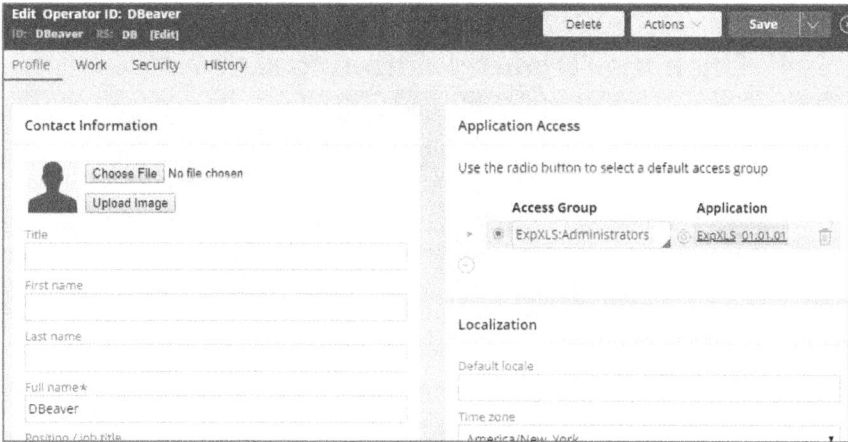

Figure 15: Sample of DBeaver With ExpXLS:Administrators Access Group

History tab

As a best practice, it is always good to provide some documentation in the "*History*" tab, as shown below.

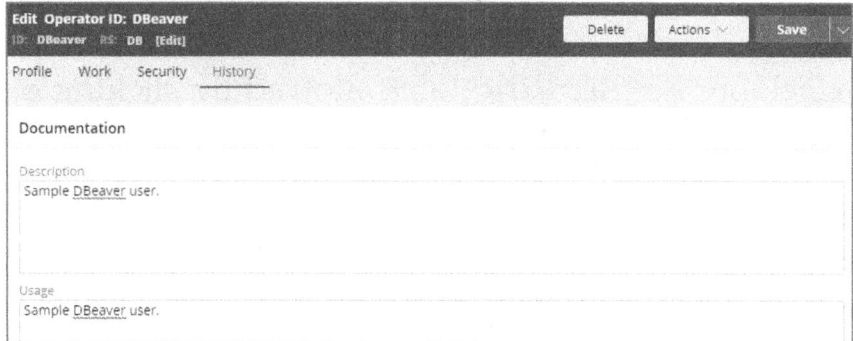

Figure 16: History Tab for DBeaver Operator ID

Work Tab

Follow the following steps to configure the *"Organizational unit"*:

1) Click on the "*Work*" tab
2) In the "*Routing*" section, click on the "*Update*" button beside the "*Organization unit*"
3) In the popup dialog, navigate and select the "*Unit*" under "*DB > Div > Unit*"
4) Click the "*Update*" button to save

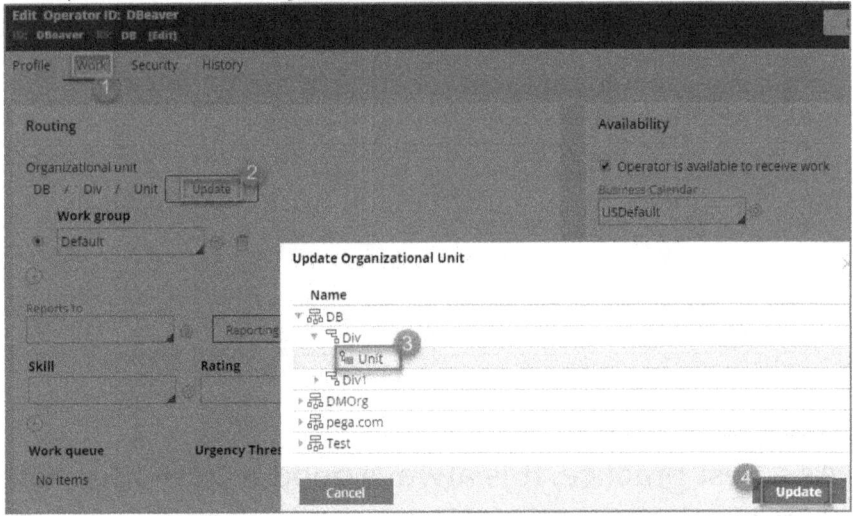

Figure 17: Update Operator Organizational Unit

Security tab

Click on the "*Security*" tab, followed by clicking on the "*Update password*" button.

Exporting Data to Excel

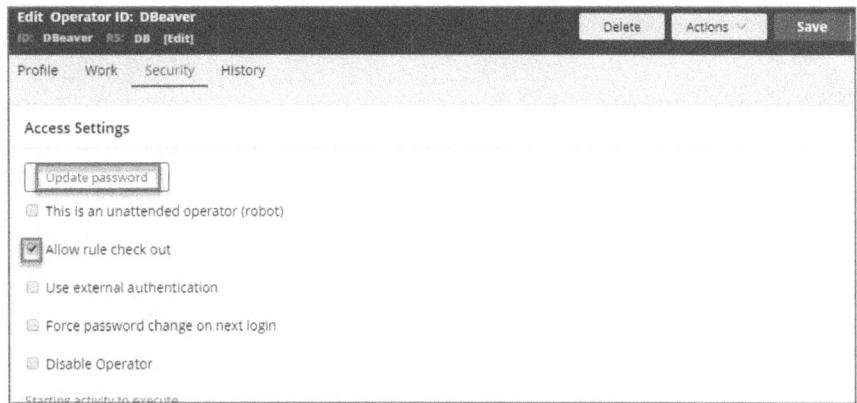

Figure 18: Sample of DBeaver Access Settings

In the dialog that popup as shown:

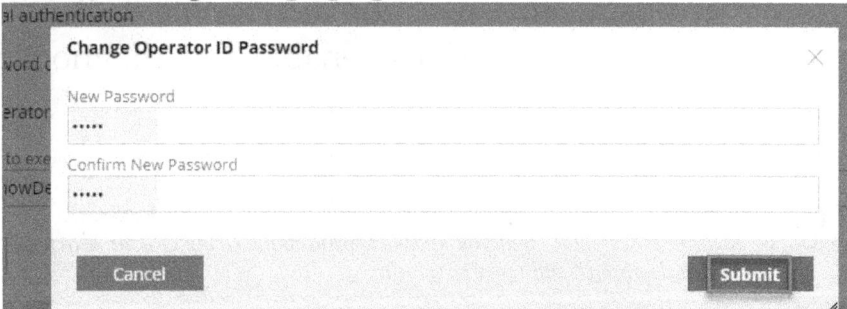

Figure 19: Changing Operator ID Password

Enter "*rules*" for both the highlighted fields above. After that, click the "*Submit*" button.

 Note:
Changing the password to [rules] is solely for convenience and demonstration purposes.

Back in the "*Security*" tab, optionally, you may tick the "*Allow rule check out*" if you desired.

Once you have made all the changes, click on the "*Save*" button to save the changes.

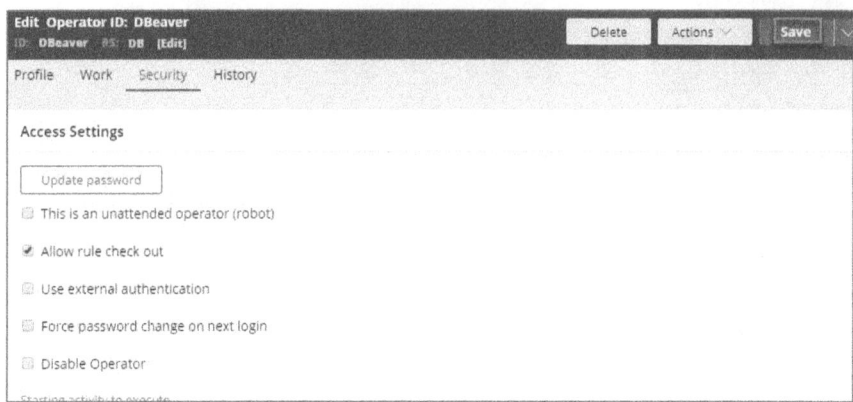

Figure 20: Saving Operator ID Changes

Enable Diagnostic Features

As we are using this user for development, it will make our life easier if we enable the diagnostic features.

 Note:
Remember the "old:" that you always append to the string of your searches? That is deprecated and replaced with this.

To do that, click on the Operator icon (the "*D*" in my case), followed by clicking on the "***Preferences***" as shown below:

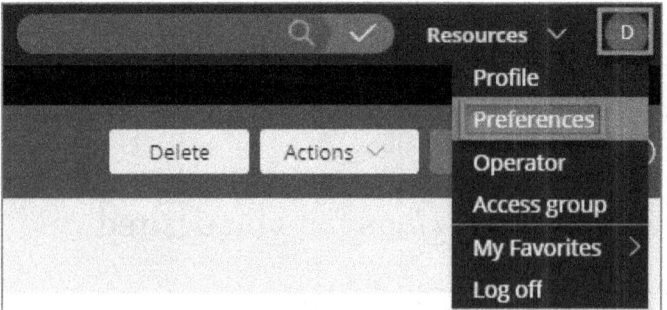

Figure 21: Launching Operator Preferences

In the dialog that opens, scroll to the bottom, and tick the "*Enable diagnostic features*". After that, click the "*Save*" button.

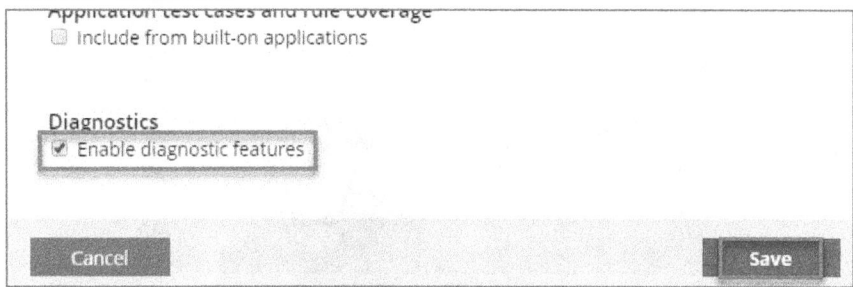

Figure 22: Enabling Diagnostic Features

 Note:
Once you are back in the Operator ID screen, remember to click the "Save" button to save the changes again.

Testing the DBeaver User

First, logout from the current operator by clicking on the operator icon on the top right, followed by clicking on the "*Log off*", as shown below.

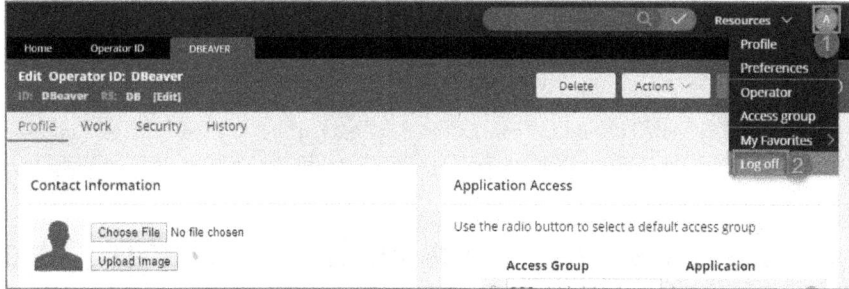

Figure 23: Logout from Pega

After logout, by default, you would be presented with the login screen. Enter the "*DBeaver*" username and its corresponding password [*rules*], followed by clicking on the "*Log in*" button.

45

Figure 24: Login as DBeaver

The most important thing that you need to validate after login is that the "*Application*" shown should relate to your newly added application access group, as shown below.

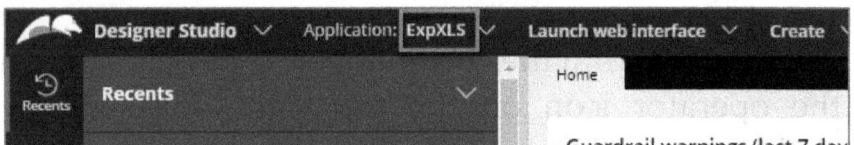

Figure 25: Sample Showing ExpXLS Selected as the Current Application

Note:
If the given user has multiple application access groups, you will need to click on the current application, followed by navigating to "Switch Application" and then clicking on your desired application to switch to.

Grant Existing User with Access to The New Application

In the top right corner of Designer Studio, do the following:

1) Enter "*DBeaver*" in the search box
2) Click on the search button

Figure 26: Searching for DBeaver Operator ID

In the search result below, click on the "*DBeaver*".

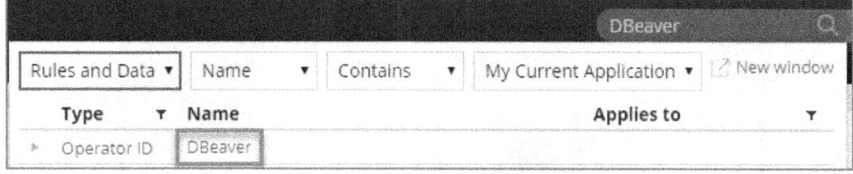
Figure 27: Search Results for Operator ID

With the Operator ID rule opened, perform the following:
1) Click on the "**+**" icon to add a new Access Group
2) In the new row of Access Group, enter the access group as: "***ExpXLS:Administrators***"
3) Click the Radio button beside this new access group to set it as the default
4) Click the "*Save*" button to save the profile

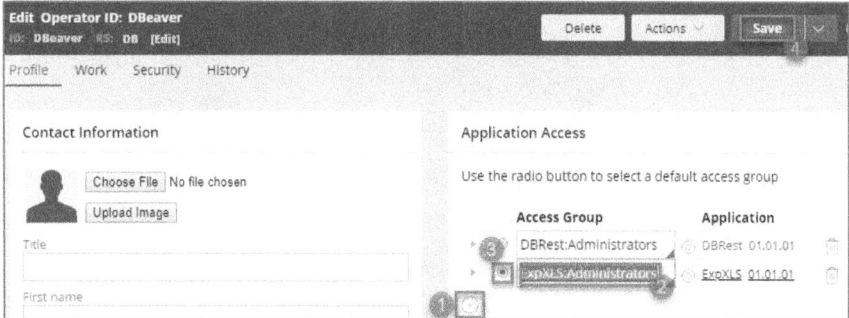
Figure 28: Example of Adding "ExpXLS:Administrators" Access Group to Existing Operator

Once saved, logout from the current user and then login as "*DBeaver*".

Once login, apart from the default application, you should also see a list of other applications that "*DBeaver*" can switch to, as shown below.

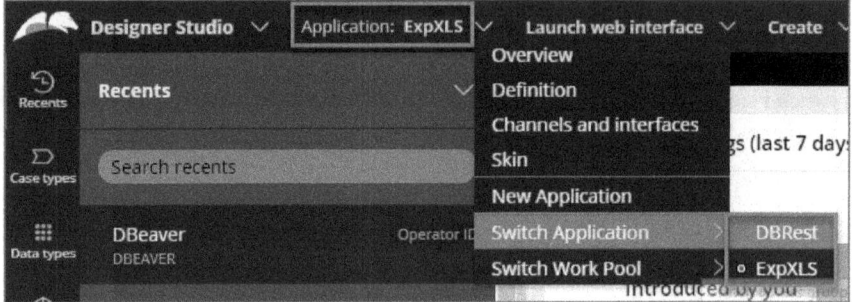

Figure 29: Example of DBeaver With 2 Application Access Groups

Creating Case Type, Flow & Section

With the groundwork done, we will now create a new Case Type, called: "*Show Users*". This Case Type basically creates an instance of the work and display a list of users in the current system, which we will export to Excel.

Login as "*DBeaver*" and ensure that the current application is "*ExpXLS*".

To create a new case type, perform the following:
1) Click on the "*Case types Explorer*"
2) Click on the "*+ Add a case type*" link
3) In the popup dialog that opens, enter "*Show Users*"
4) Click the "*Submit*" button

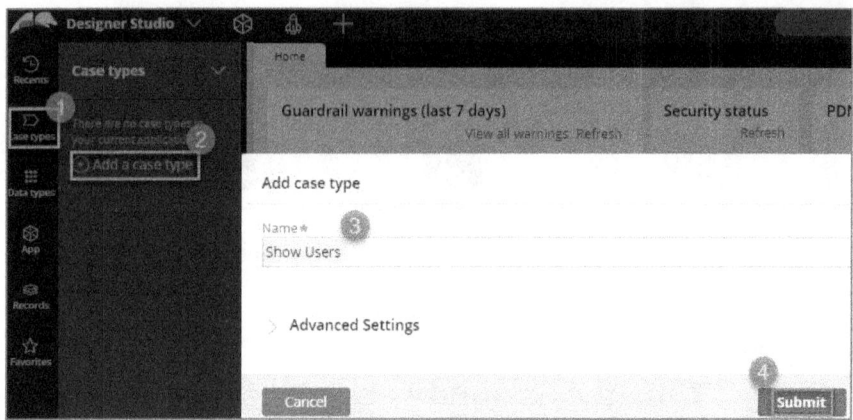

Figure 30: Creating a Show Users Case Type

In the form that opens, click on "*Workflow*" tab, followed by the "*Add life cycle*" button.

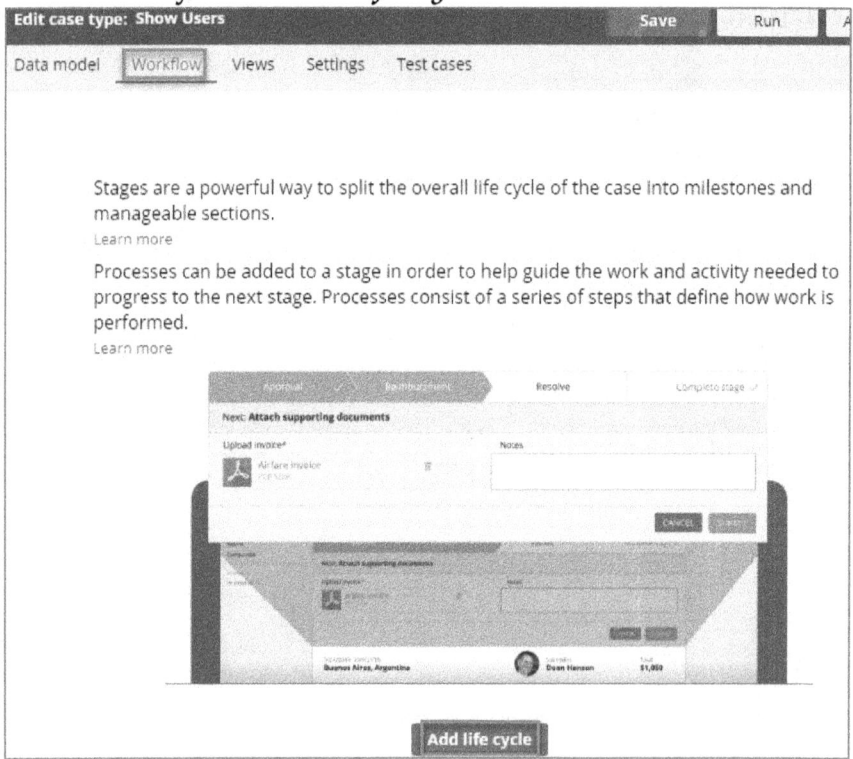

Figure 31: Adding Life Cycle for the Show Users Case Type

The screen will now show the "*Case life cycle*" and the stages.

Perform the following to create a new process and step:
1) Enter "*Data Query*" as the stage name
2) Click on the "*+ STEP*"
3) In the options, click on the "*Collect information*"

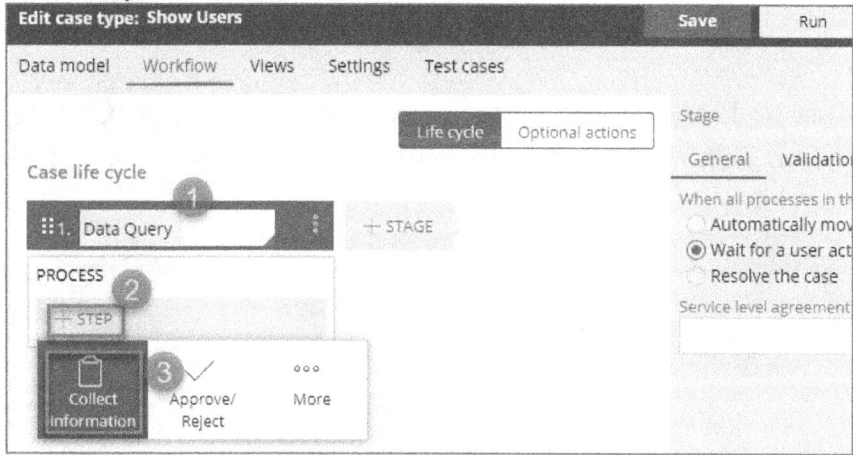

Figure 32: Creating a New Stage, Process and Step

Next, change the step name to "*List Users*", followed by clicking on the "*Save*" button.

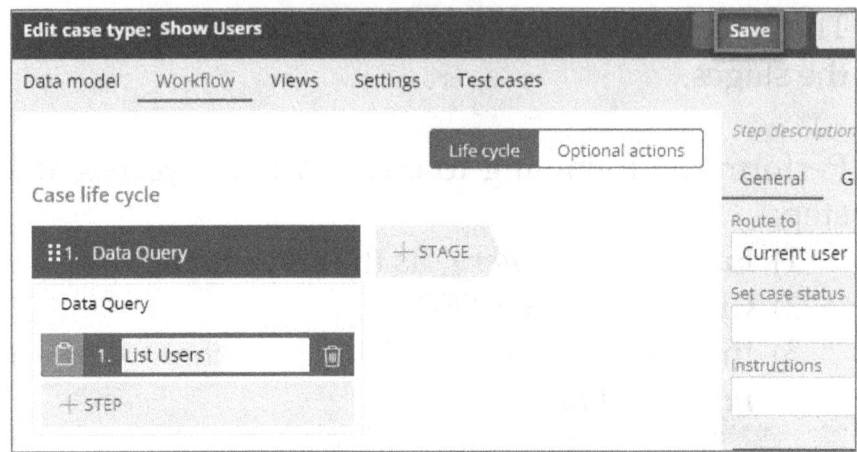

Figure 33: Updating the Step Name

Go to the "*Settings*" tab and tick the "*Skip 'Create' view when users create a new case*". After that, click the "*Save*" button.

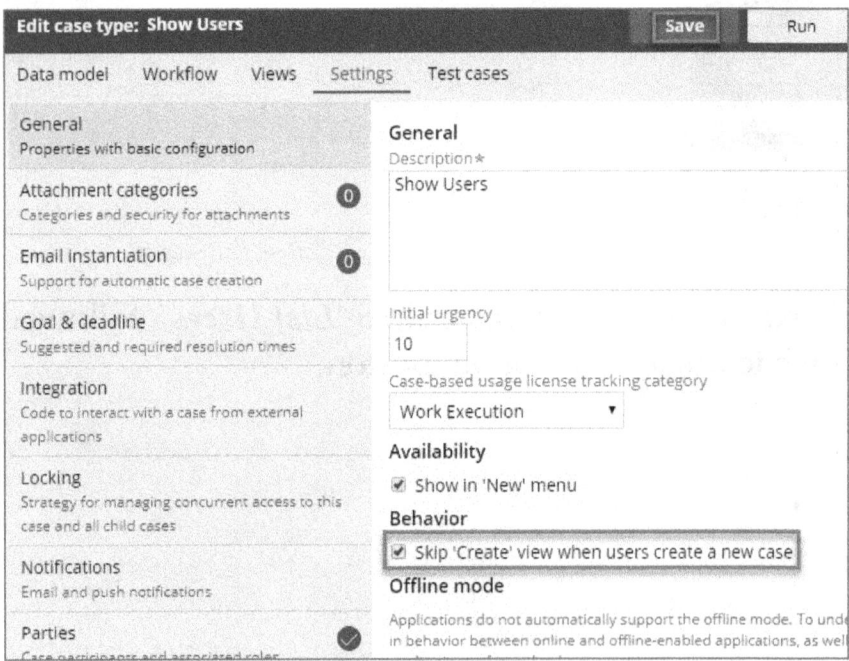

Figure 34: Skip 'Create' View When Creating a New Case

Back in the "*Workflow*" tab, click on the "*Data Query*" process, followed by the "*Open process*" button on the right.

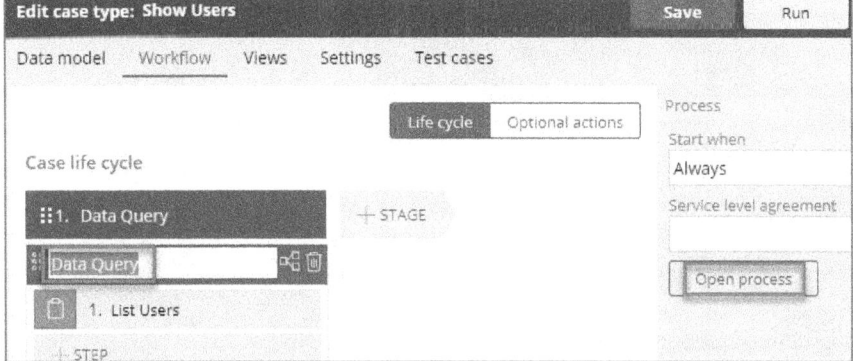

Figure 35: Opening a Process

In the opened process, right-click on the "*List Users*" link and select the "*View Properties*" context menu item.

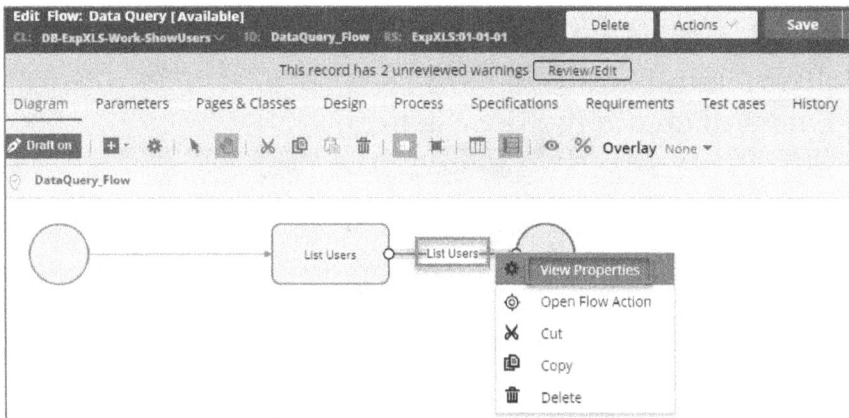

Figure 36: Inspecting Flow Action Properties

In the opened dialog box, click on the icon on the right of the "*ListUsers*" Flow action, as shown below.

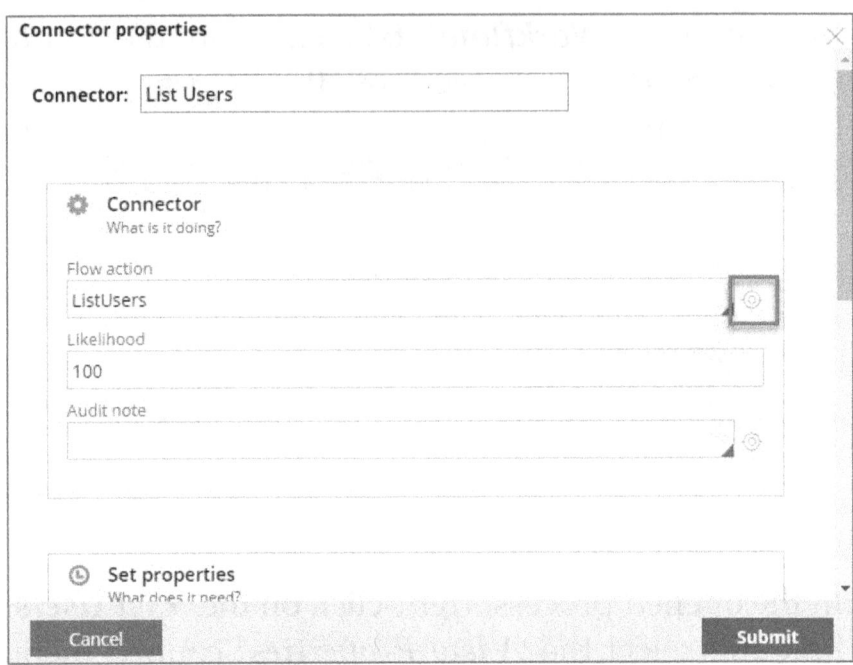

Figure 37: Creating a Flow Action In Process Flow

In the "*Create Flow Action*" form, take the default as shown below and click the "*Create and open*" button. This will create the flow action.

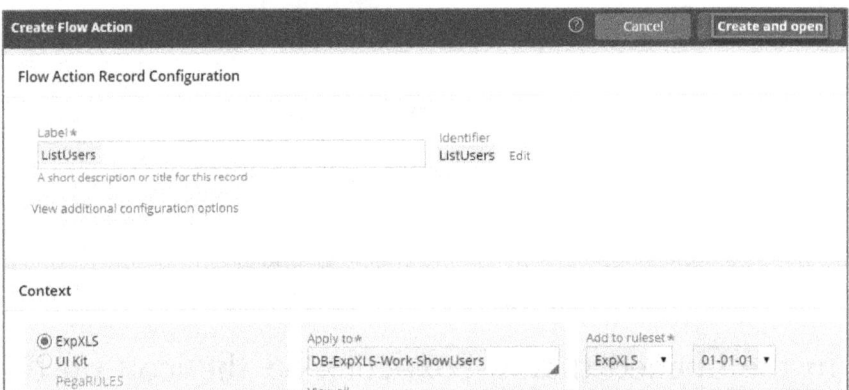

Figure 38: Creating a Flow Action

In the flow action screen shown below, under the "*Section*" field, give it the same name as the flow action, i.e. "*ListUsers*". After that, click the icon on its right to create this section rule.

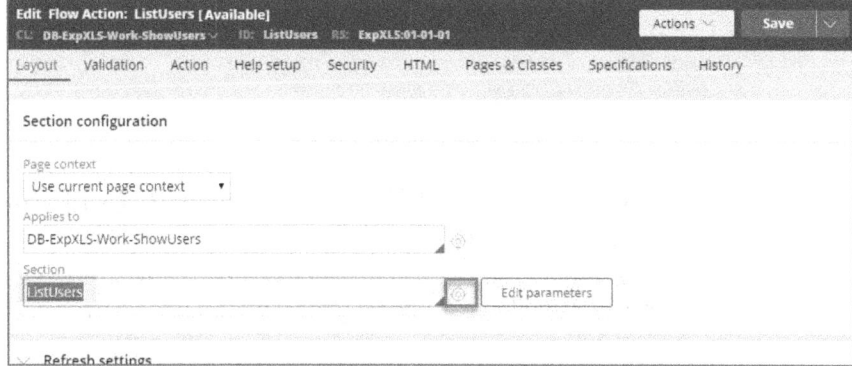

Figure 39: Creating a Section In Flow Action

In the "*Create Section*" screen below, take all the defaults and click the "*Create and open*" button to create the section.

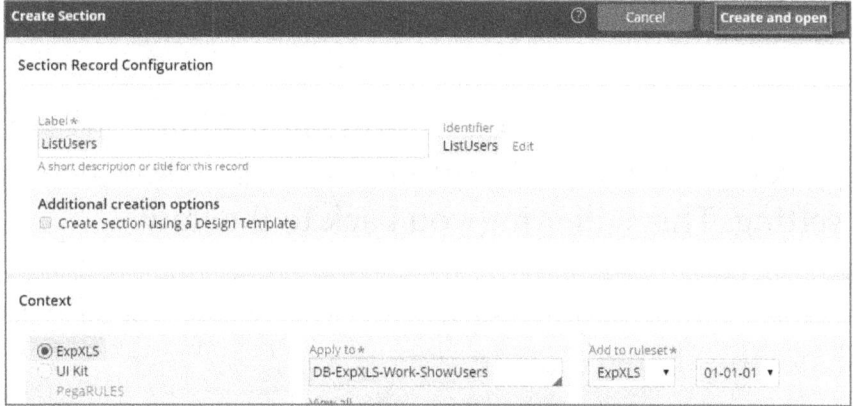

Figure 40: Create Section Screen

When the section opens, click the "*Save*" button to save this blank section first.

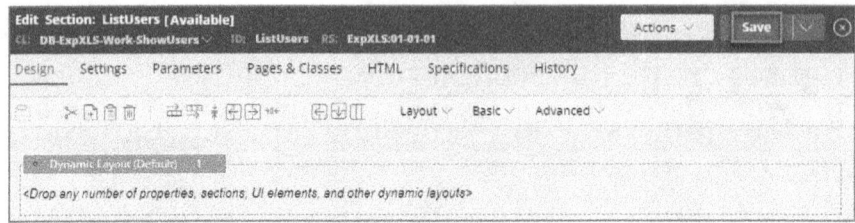

Figure 41: Saving a Section

Go back to the "*ListUsers*" Flow Action and click on the "*Save*" button.

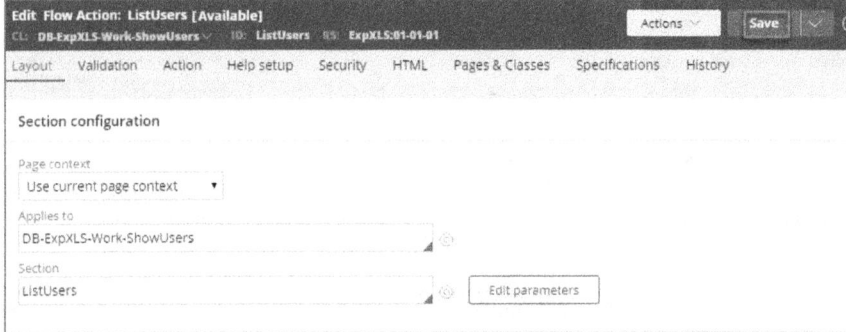

Figure 42: Saving a Flow Action

Similarly, go back to the "*DataQuery_Flow*" process, click on the "*Submit*" button to save the Flow Action setting. This will bring you back to the flow.

Back in the flow screen, click the "*Save*" button to save the changes made.

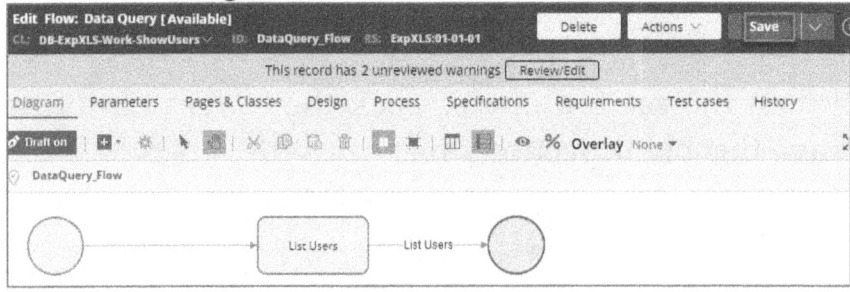

Figure 43: Saving a Flow

At this point, we have created a simple framework for us to implement the actual stuff.

Modifying the UI to List Data

In this chapter, we will modify the section of the "*List Users*" step to run a report definition to list the users of the system. At the same time, add 2 buttons for exporting the data using the 1st Method and the 2nd Method, respectively.

Ensure that you are login as "*DBeaver*", with the current application as "*ExpXLS*".

Reusing the Existing Report Definition (RD)

As highlighted before, we will reuse an existing RD. In this case, let us use "*pyGetListOfOperators*".

In the *Master Beaver Version*, we will be making modifications to this RD, therefore, we might as well save it into our application ruleset now.

In the following "*pyGetListOfOperators*" RD, click on the "*Save as*" button.

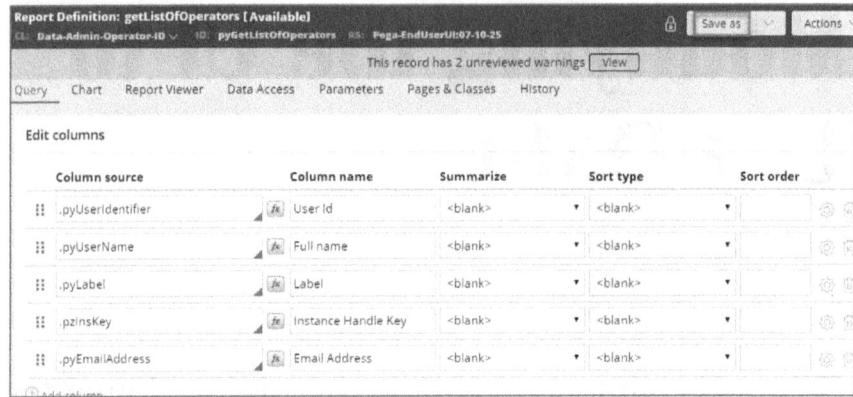

Figure 44: The OOTB pyGetListOfOperators Report Definition

In the following screen, check that the info is as displayed and click the "*Create and open*" button.

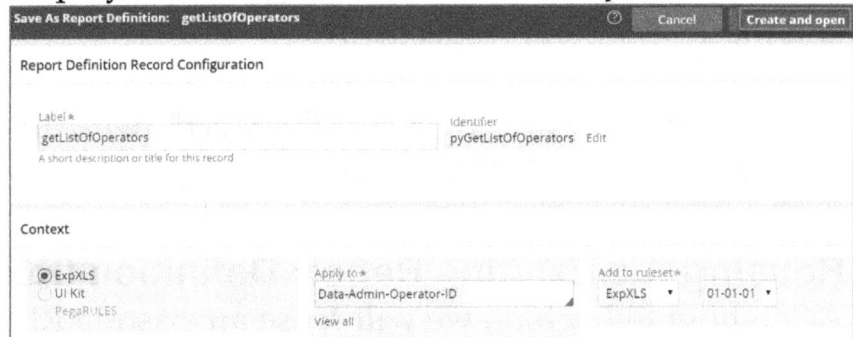

Figure 45: Saving a Copy of the RD Into Our Ruleset

Verify that the RD is saved into our ruleset as shown below.

Exporting Data to Excel

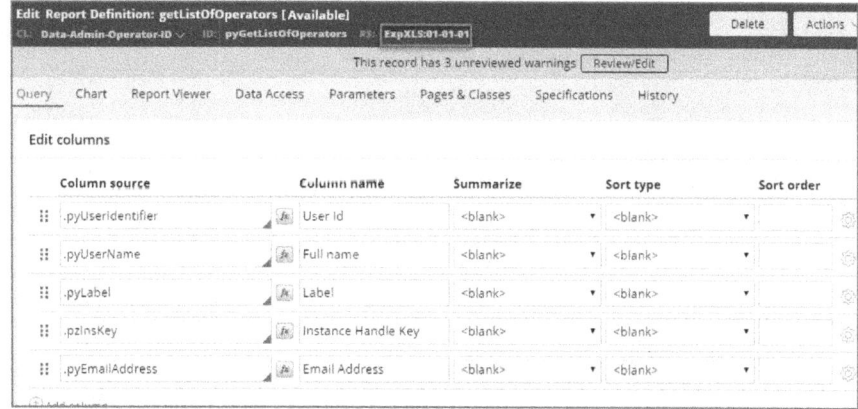

Figure 46: The OOB Ruleset Saved Into Our ruleset

Modifying the "*ListUsers*" Section

Ensure that the earlier section, "*ListUsers*", is opened for modification, as shown below.

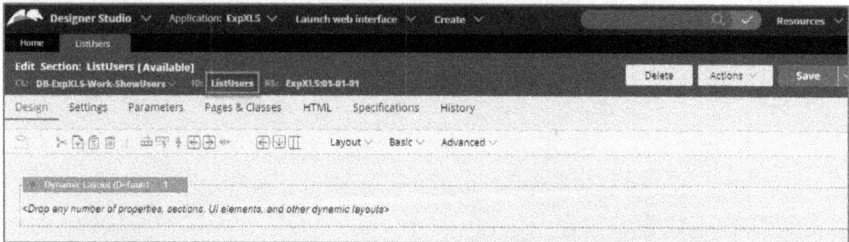

Figure 47: ListUsers Section Ready for Modifications

In this section, click the "*Layout*" menu, followed by dragging and dropping the "*Table*" into the section's "*Dynamic Layout*" area.

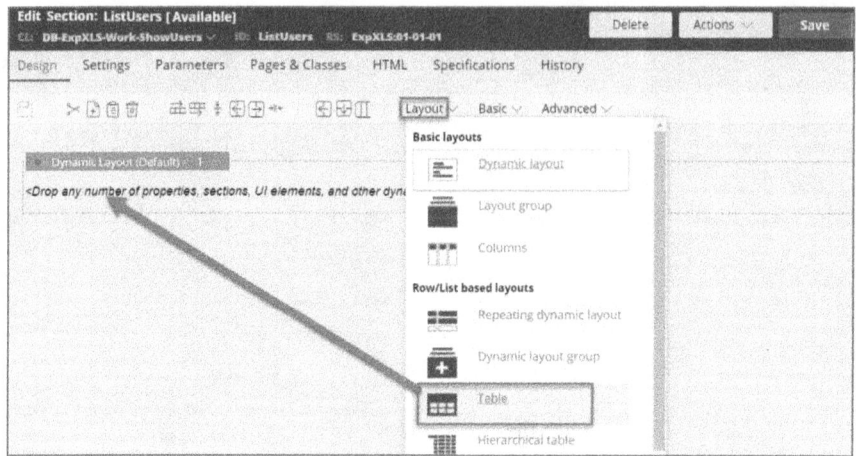

Figure 48: Adding a Table to a Section

If you do it correctly, you will see the table as highlighted below.

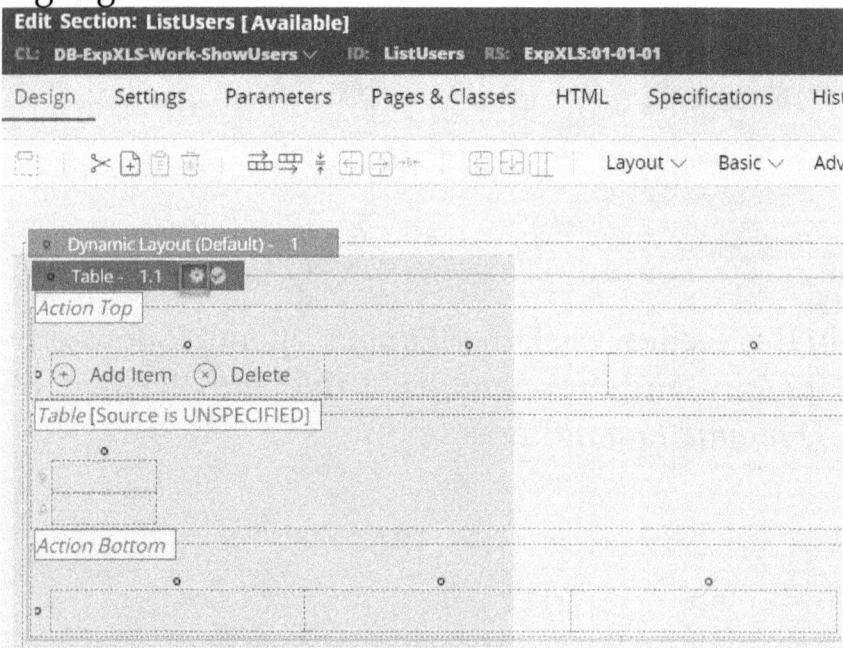

Figure 49: Table Within A Dynamic Layout

Click on the marked icon above to open the "*Layout Properties*", and configure the "*General*" tab as shown here:
- Source: ***Report Definition***
- Applies To: ***Data-Admin-Operator-ID***
- Report definition: ***pyGetListOfOperators***
- Tick the "*Create grid dynamically*"

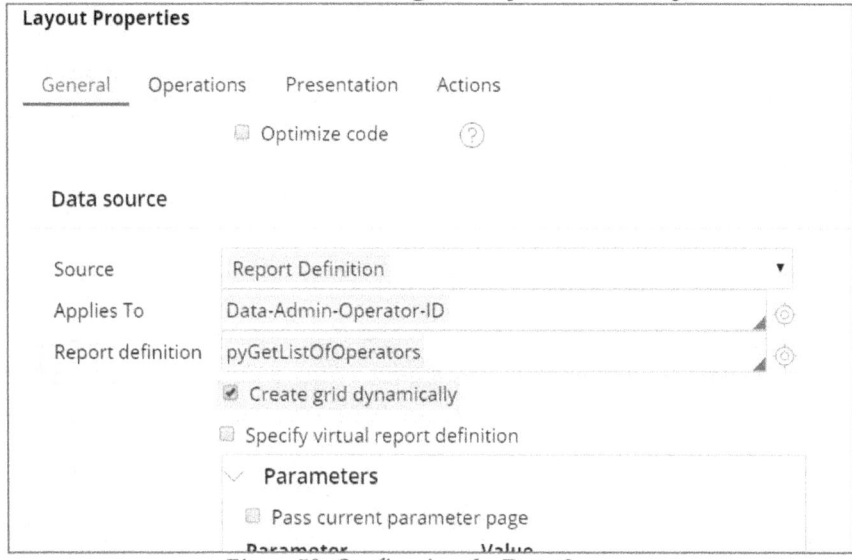

Figure 50: Configuring the Data Source

Scroll to the bottom, and under the "*Header and footer*", untick both the "*Display grid header*" and "*Display grid footer*". After that, click the "*Submit*" button to proceed.

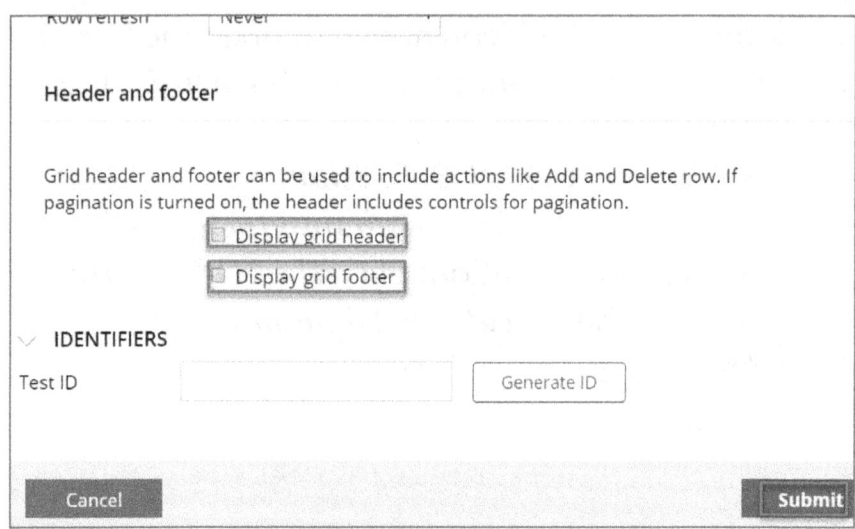

Figure 51: Untick the Grid Header and Footer

Your section should now look like the following. Click the "*Save*" button.

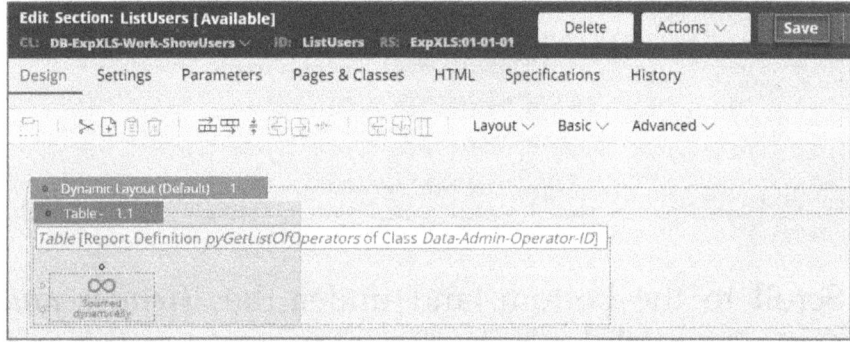

Figure 52: Table with Report Definition Configured Dynamically

Testing the Listing

Click on the "*Launch web interface*", followed by the "*Case Worker*" menu item to launch the "**Case Worker Portal**".

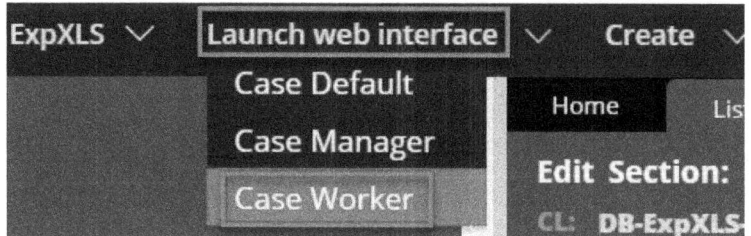
Figure 53: Launching the Case Worker Portal

In the "*Case Worker Portal*", click on "*New*", followed by the "*Show Users*" Case Type.

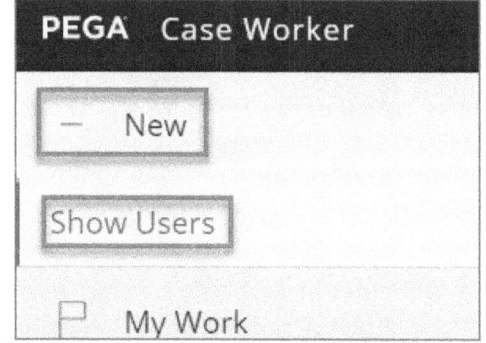
Figure 54: Launching a Case Type in Case Worker

If everything goes well, you should see the following, listing the users of the system.

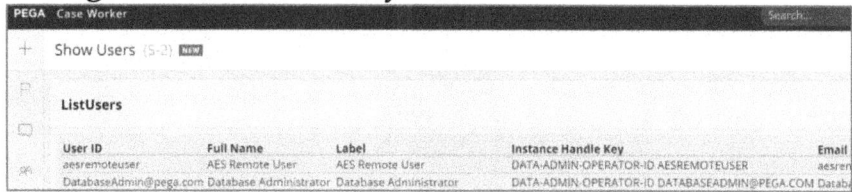
Figure 55: Listing of Users in the System

Part 2: Exporting Data to Excel

Introducing Method 1: Using Predefined Excel Template

This is the most commonly described method on the Internet, and it requires the following:
- Create an Excel file template, with a predefined format to represent the data fields to be exported
- Add a button in the section to call a script function and include the script in the harness
- Implement the script function to invoke an activity
- Implement the activity to call Pega Excel generation activity, *MSOGenerateExcelFile*, passing in the earlier Excel template as a parameter

Once the above is done, you can proceed to test it out.

In the next chapter, we will go into the details of implementing each of those above.

Method 1: Creating Excel File Template

Create an Excel file with the following columns and values:

Column	values
User Id	{.pxResults().pyUserIdentifier input}
Full name	{.pxResults().pyUserName input}
Label	{.pxResults().pyLabel input}
Instance Handle Key	{.pxResults().pzInsKey input}
Email Address	{.pxResults().pyEmailAddress input}

Figure 56: Excel Template Columns and Values

The following is how the Excel template looks like:

	A	B	C	
1	User Id	Full name	Label	Inst
2	{.pxResults().pyUserIdentifier input}	{.pxResults().pyUserName input}	{.pxResults().pyLabel input}	{.px
3				

Figure 57: Snapshot of the Excel Template

Now, name the Excel file as:
- "*DBeaverExcelExport.xlsx*".

Upload the Template as a Binary File

To create a new Binary File, perform the following:
1) Click on the "*Records Explorer*"
2) Expand the "*Technical*"

3) Right-click on "*Binary File*"
4) Click on "*Create*"

The following shows the menu navigation:

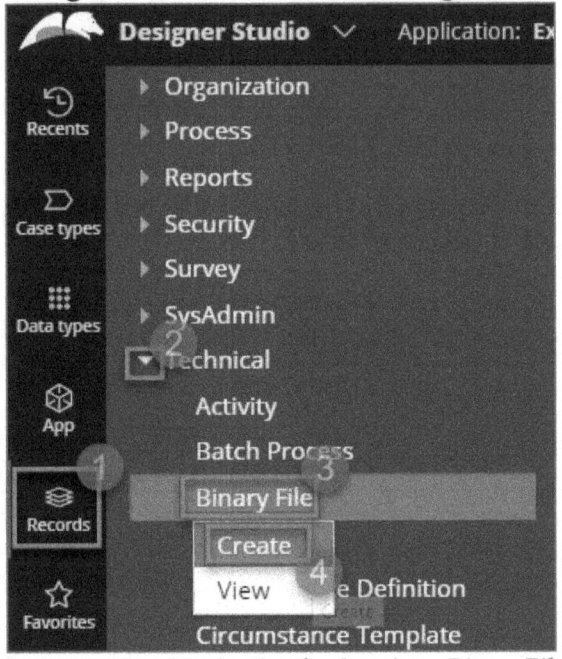

Figure 58: Menu Navigation for Creating a Binary File

With the opened form enter the info as follows, followed by clicking on the "*Create and open*".

Exporting Data to Excel

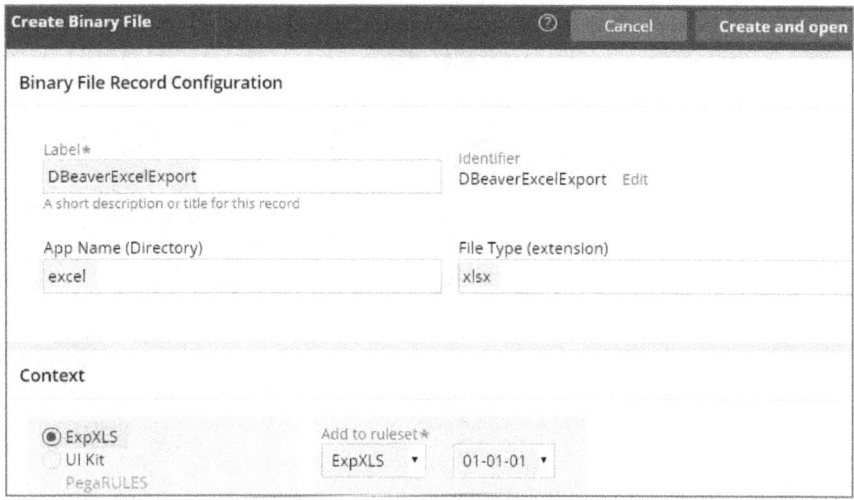

Figure 59: Creating a Binary File

In the following screen, to upload a file, perform the following:

1) Click on the "*Upload file*" button
2) In the "*Upload file*" dialog, select the "*DBeaverExcelExport.xlsx*" file,
3) Click on the "*Upload file*" button to upload

The following screen shows the steps.

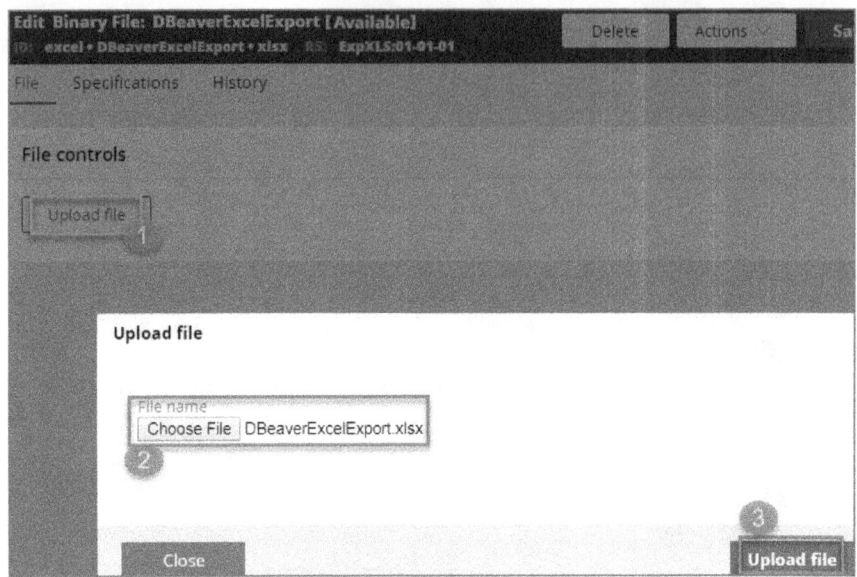
Figure 60: Uploading a Binary File

Back in the Binary File page, click on the "*Save*" button to save.

Method 1: Adding a Button In Section

The next step is to add a button to invoke the Excel export. Since we are going to implement both methods, let us add both buttons now.

The following is an example of the new section.

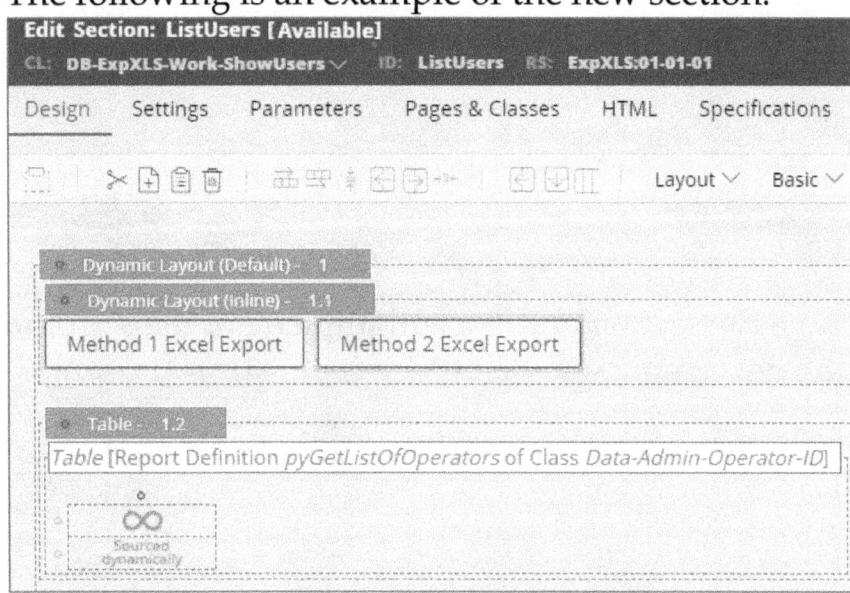

Figure 61: Section With Buttons Added

For the "*Method 1 Excel Export*" button, add the on-click event to run the "*DoExcelExport*" script, with 3 parameters as shown below:

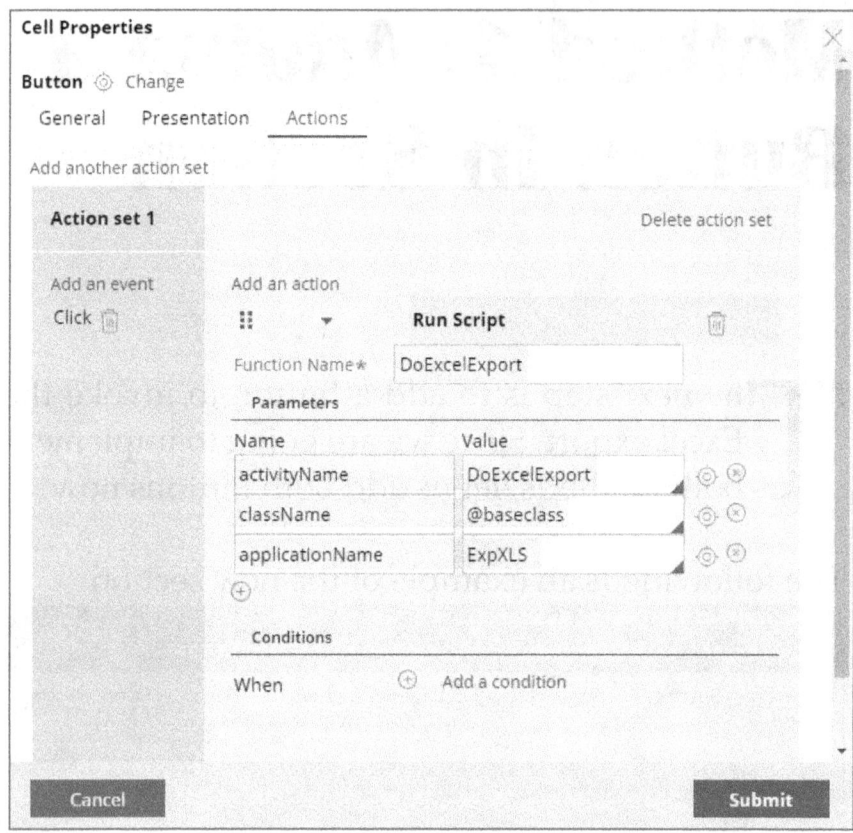

Figure 62: Actions Tab Configuration

Save the section and we will implement the script in the next step.

Method 1: Creating the Script

The script that we will be creating is basically a javascript file. This script will take in the inputs mentioned in the above chapter and then calls an activity.

Perform the following to create a new text file:
1) Go to "*Records Explorer*"
2) Expand the "*Technical*" section
3) Right-click on the "*Text File*"
4) Click on "*Create*"

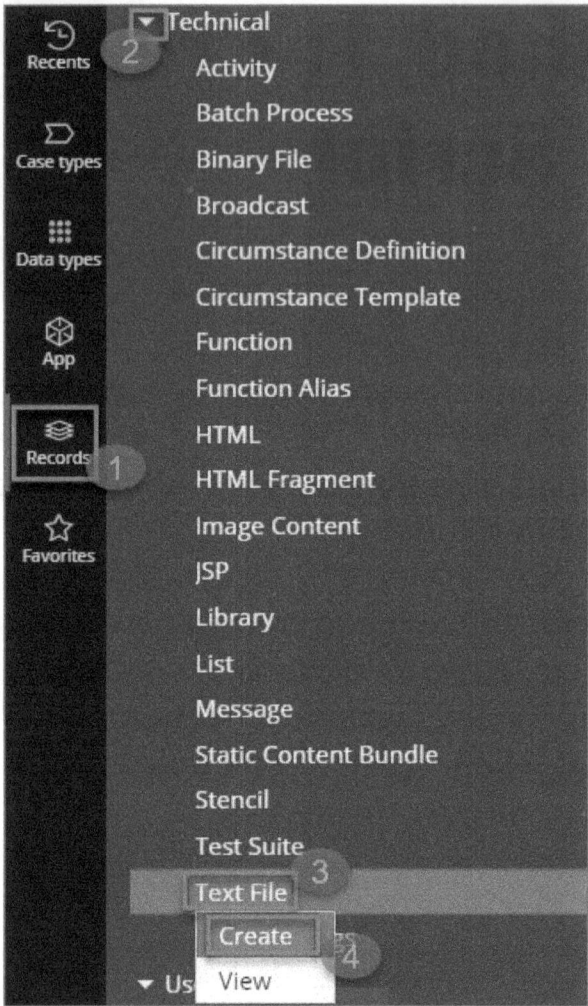

Figure 63: Navigating the Create Text File Menu Item

In the form that opens, enter as follows:

Exporting Data to Excel

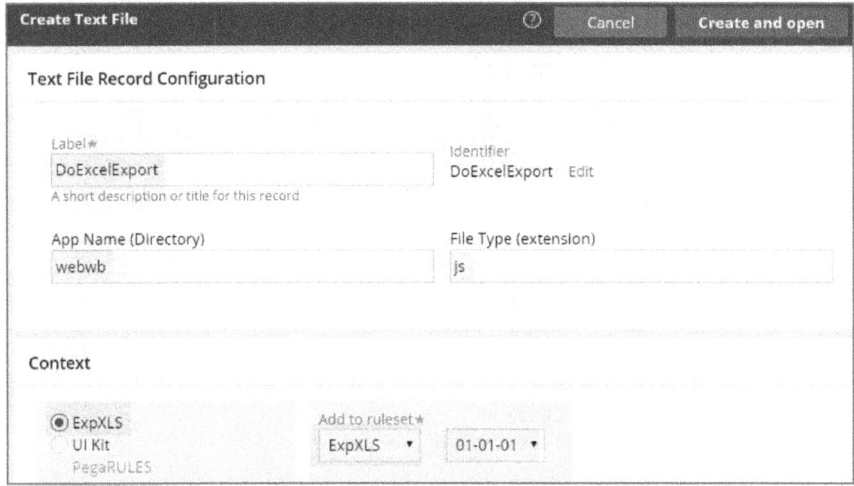

Figure 64: Creating a New Text File

Click "*Create and open*" to proceed. In the new text file, enter the following code:

```
function DoExcelExport(activityName, className, applicationName)
{
  var sURL = SafeURL_createFromURL(pega.u.d.url);
  sURL.put("pyActivity", activityName);
  sURL.put("pyClassName", className);
  sURL.put("ApplicationName", applicationName);

  var formElement = document.createElement("form");
  formElement.id = "call_activity_from_js";
  formElement.method = "POST";
  formElement.action = sURL.toURL();
  if (pega.env.ua.webkit)
    formElement.target = "";
  document.body.appendChild(formElement);
  formElement.submit();
  document.body.removeChild(formElement);
}
```

Figure 65: Javascript Code for DoExcelExport

 Note:
Instead of typing all the codes, you can go to DebunkumBeaver.com website to copy it.

79

The following is the screenshot of the completed *DoExcelExport* javascript:

```
function DoExcelExport(activityName, className, applicationName)
{
    var sURL = SafeURL_createFromURL(pega.u.d.url);
    sURL.put("pyActivity", activityName);
    sURL.put("pyClassName", className);
    sURL.put("ApplicationName", applicationName);

    var formElement = document.createElement("form");
    formElement.id = "call_activity_from_js";
    formElement.method = "POST";
    formElement.action = sURL.toURL();
    if (pega.env.ua.webkit)
       formElement.target = "";
    document.body.appendChild(formElement);
    formElement.submit();
    document.body.removeChild(formElement);
}
```

Figure 66: DoExcelExport JS File

Adding the JS Into a Harness

The javascript needs to be added to the harness for it to be available. In this case, I have saved a copy of the "***Perform***" harness into my ruleset, and added it there, as shown below.

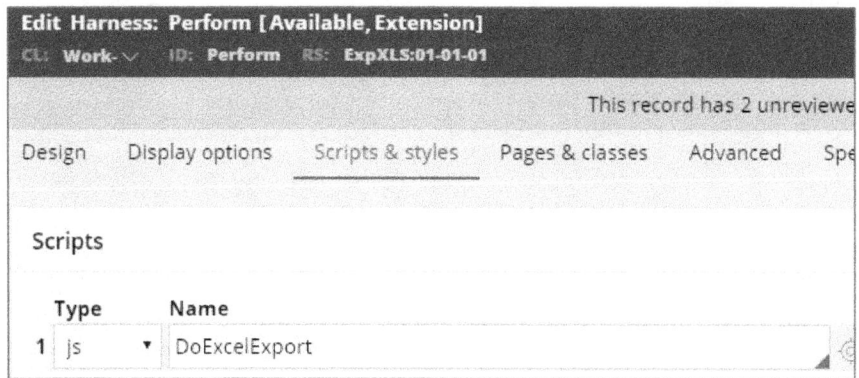
Figure 67: Adding JS to the Harness

Method 1: Creating the Activity

The last rule to create is the *DoExcelExport* activity. This activity is invoked by the javascript, which then calls the OOTB *MSOGenerateExcelFile*.

The following is the activity creation screen:

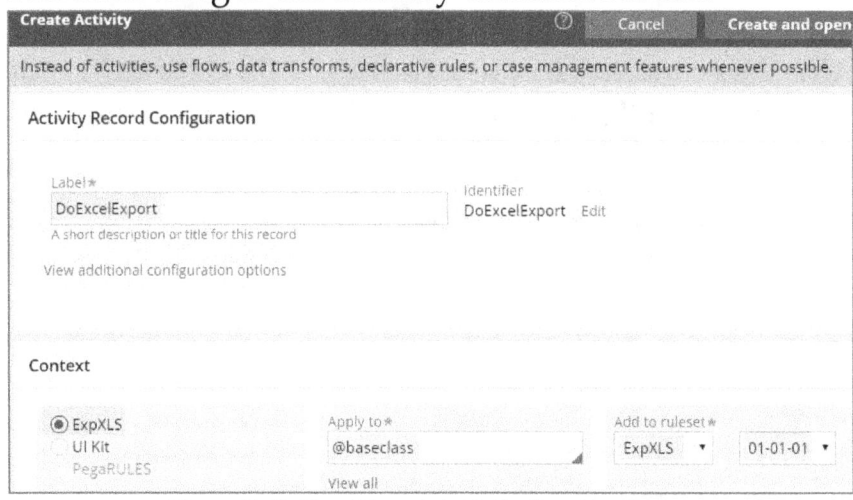

Figure 68: DoExcelExport Activity Creation Screen

In the activity, there is only 1 step. Enter the data as follows:

Method	Call MSOGenerateExcelFile
FSFileName	"GeneratedExcelData.xlsx"
TemplateRFB	"excel!DBeaverExcelExport!xlsx"
DownloadFile	[ticked]

The following shows the DoExcelExport rule:

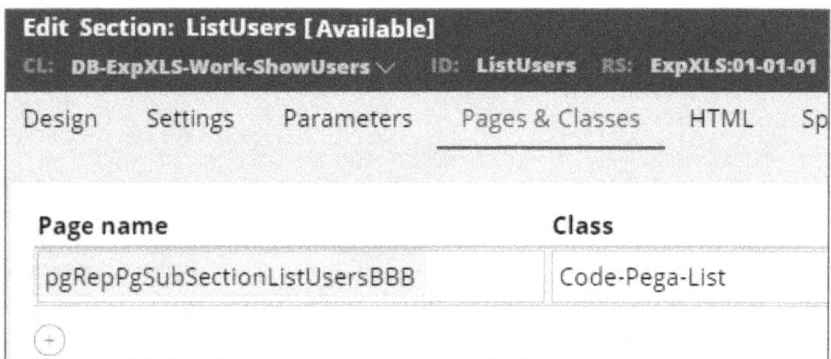

Figure 69: DoExcelExport Activity

The "*MSOGenerateExcelFile*" needs another input, the "*Page name*". In our example, this is found in the "*Pages & Classes*" of our *ListUsers* section, as follows:

Figure 70: Generated Pagename for RD

Note:
The "*pgRepPgSubSectionListUsersBBB*" is a generated Pagename for RD. Your value for this could be different, so remember to go to the "Pages & Classes" of your ListUsers section to get the actual value.

Enter that info into the "*Step page*" of the method call. The following shows the completed "*DoExcelExport*" activity.

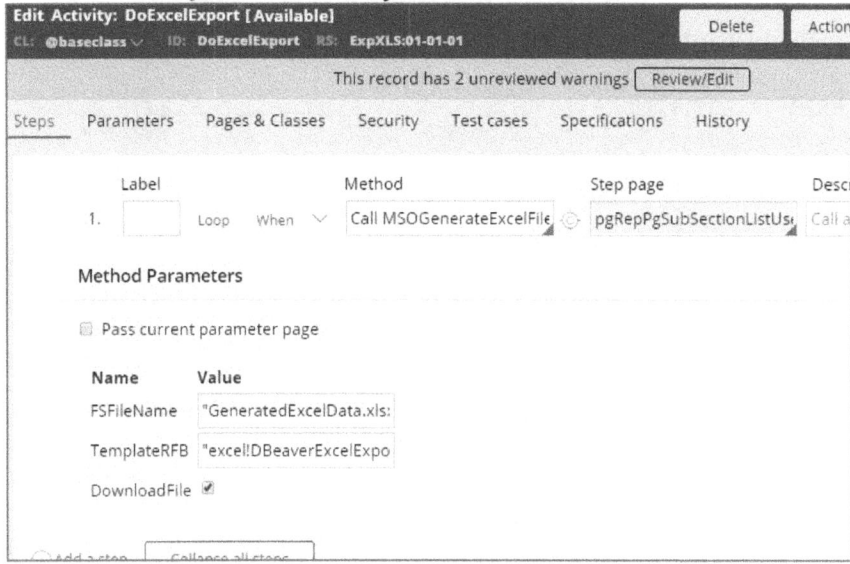

Figure 71: Updated DoExcelExport Activity (Steps Tab)

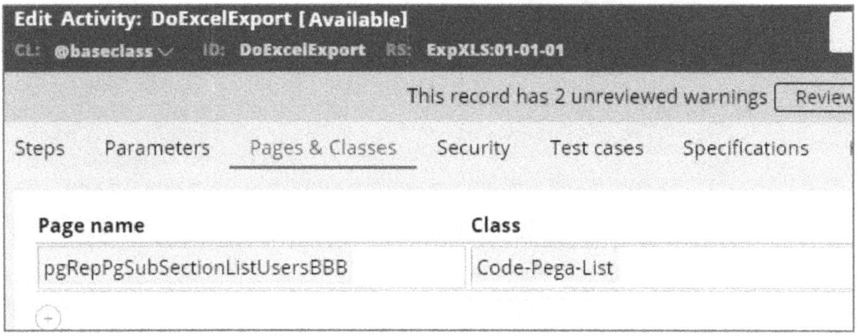

Figure 72: Updated DoExcelExport Activity (Pages & Classes Tab)

Note that due to our way of invocation, we also need to make some changes to this activity in the "*Security*" tab. For the following, tick the "*Allow direct invocation from the client or a service"* checkbox, as shown below:

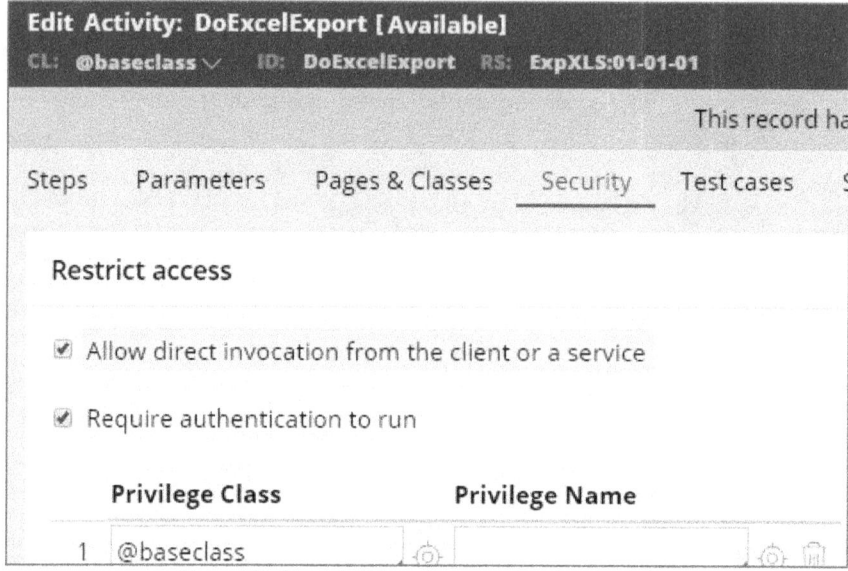

Figure 73: Enable Direct Invocation for Activity

Testing Method 1

Now, let's test the Excel export! To do that, launch the "*Case Worker Portal*", then create a new "*Show Users*" case, the following shows the listing of all the users in the system.

Figure 74: Running An Instance of the Show Users Case Type

In the above, click on the "**Method 1 Excel Export**" button, and you will see the Excel generated as shown below:

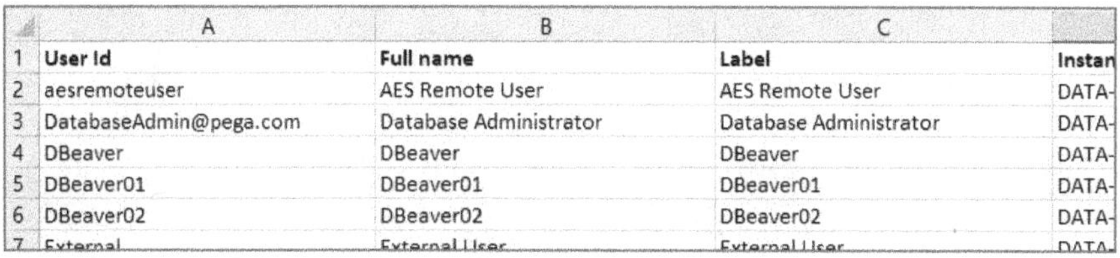

Figure 75: Exported Data In Excel Using Method 1

Pega How-to Guide

Note:
Depending on your browser settings, you may be prompted with a dialog for you to specify a Save-As location or to indicate that you want to Open it directly. Some browsers might even download it directly into a default location.

Congratulation! You have now completed the exporting of data into Excel!

Introducing Method 2: Without Any New Rules

Interestingly, there is a much easier method to export data to Excel. Not only is it easier, but it is also better in many aspects.

There are basically only 2 steps:
1) Call a script function
2) Include the required script in the harness

Most importantly, there is no need for you to create any new rules!

Method 2: Calling the Script Function

While login as "*DBeaver*", open the section, "*ListUsers*", that we created earlier. Remember that we had created the 2nd button?

Now, for the click event of that button, add an action of "*Run Script*", with the following details:

Function Name:
`"pega.report.commandribbon.exportToExcel"`
Parameters:

Page	`pgRepPgSubSectionListUsersBBB`
obj	`script:this`
event	`script:event`

The following shows the completed settings of the "*Actions*" tab.

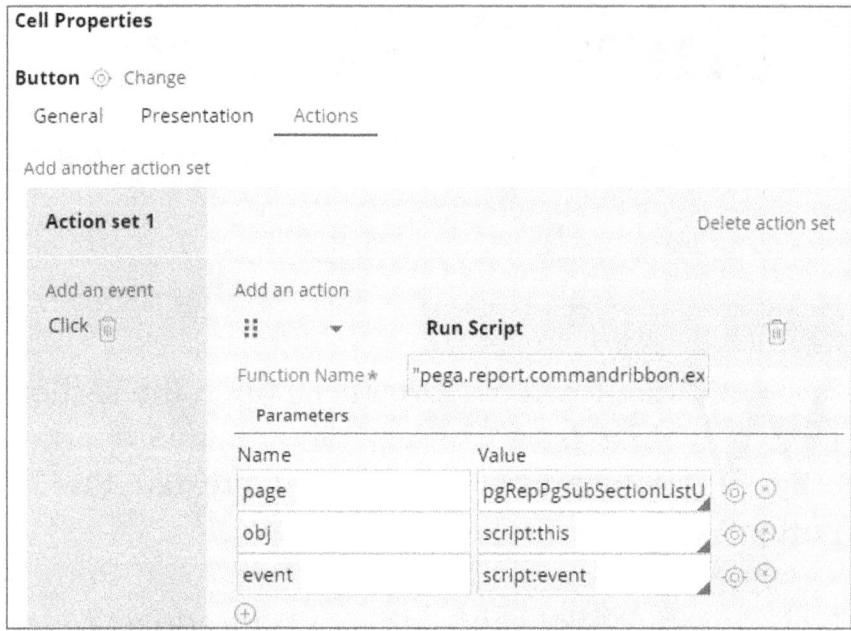

Figure 76: Settings in the Actions Tab for Invoking Excel Export

Note:
Remember the "pgRepPgSubSectionListUsersBBB"? In the earlier chapters, we had mentioned that it is a generated Pagename for RD. Your value for this could be different, so remember to use the right one. You can refer to "Figure 70: Generated Pagename for RD" for more info.

Once you have made the changes and saved, you can proceed to the next chapter.

Method 2: Including the Required Script

Remember that we had earlier added a script in the *Perform* harness? We shall add one more script to that.

The script to add is:
pzPega_report_commandribbon.js

The following is the screenshot of the harness with the added script.

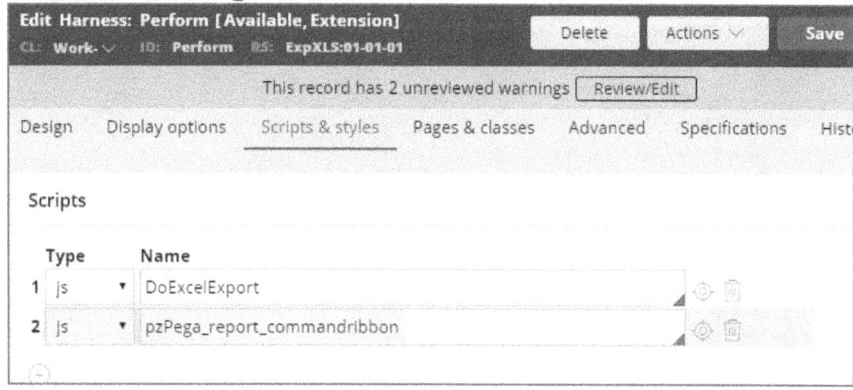

Figure 77: Scripts & Styles Tab of Harness

After adding the script, save this harness.

Testing Method 2

Yes, you are right… it is done… and we can test it now! Bear in mind that the steps for method 2 is so short and simple NOT because we are reusing the work done in Method 1, it is just that it is really that simple!

Now, launch the "*Case Worker Portal*", start a case, and then click on the "*Method 2 Excel Report*" button.

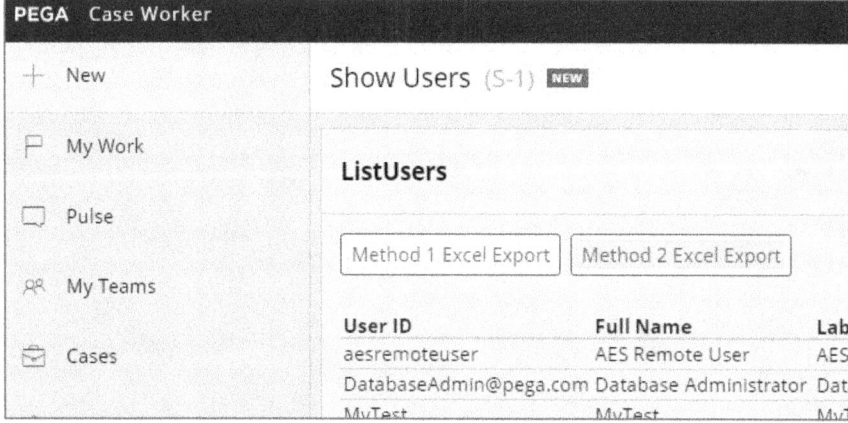

Figure 78: Method 2 Excel Export Button Implemented

The Excel generated will then be available to you! The following is the screenshot of the generated Excel.

User ID	Full Name	Label	Instanc
aesremoteuser	AES Remote User	AES Remote User	DATA-A
DatabaseAdmin@pega.com	Database Administrator	Database Administrator	DATA-A
DBeaver	DBeaver	DBeaver	DATA-A
DBeaver01	DBeaver01	DBeaver01	DATA-A
DBeaver02	DBeaver02	DBeaver02	DATA-A
External	External User	External User	DATA-A

Figure 79: Exported Data In Excel Using Method 2

Note:
Remember once again, depending on your browser settings, you may be prompted with a dialog for you to specify a Save-As location or to indicate that you want to Open it directly. Some browsers might even download it directly into a default location.

Method 2 is interestingly simple and cool, isn't it?

Summary

Both Method 1 and Method 2 achieved the same outcome – export data to Excel.

However, Method 1 is far more complex and much less maintainable than Method 2.

It is interesting to note that in practice, Method 1 is more often implemented than Method 2.

In this *Pega How-to Guide: Exporting Data to Excel*, I had intentionally walked you through both Method 1 and Method 2, so that you could see the difference: a 'hacking' method vs a graceful one.

Pega is a great tool, it is fast and powerful, provided that you use it correctly.

A simple task such as exporting data to Excel takes less than 2 minutes to implement; however, if done wrongly, it could take days, at the same time, create so much unnecessary complexity!

This is also one of the reasons why I had decided to launch the *Pega How-to Guide* series. This is not an easy endeavour, but a necessary one – if we want a better adoption rate for Pega, as well as a better Pega implementation.

With that, let us move on to the Master Beaver Discussion, in which I will explain and show you some inherent limitations of those methods. This will help to elevate your knowledge and improve your appreciation of Pega, as well as to be able to use this knowledge in your specific project situations.

 Note: This is a How-to Version, only highlights from the Master Beaver Discussion are provided.

Part 3: Master Beaver Discussion

[This How-to Version has outlines ONLY]

Adding A New Reporting Field

Now, let's evaluate the impact of changing the listing. For this case, let us add an Update time field from the Operator ID table to the listing and investigate the impact.

Modify the Report Definition

Figure 80: Added a DateTime Field in Report Definition

Figure 81: Section is Automatically Updated with the New Column

Note:
The section was able to automatically update the listing because we had ticked the "Create grid dynamically" checkbox earlier in Figure 50: Configuring the Data Source.

Fixing the Date Format for the UI Display

Figure 82: Configuring RD Field Formatting

Figure 83: Specifying the DateTime Format

> **Note:**
> The formatting, such as Day/Month or Month/Day, etc., still depends on your user locale. To change that, go to your operator profile, under the "Localization", enter an appropriate value in the "Default locale" field, such as "en_US", "en_AU", etc.. Please note that you also need to logout from the Designer Studio for the changes to take effect.
>
> If you want the format to be consistent across all users, you can select the "DateTime Format as "Custom" and then entering your own format.

Figure 84: Update Time Column with Proper Formatting in the UI

Method 1 Generation with New Column

Figure 85: Generated Excel Using Method 1 After New Column Added

Method 2 Generation with New Column

Figure 86: Generated Excel Using Method 2 After New Column Added

> **Note:**
> The formatting for the Update Time in the Excel is independent with the report definition, i.e. even without setting the date formatting in the report definition, the formatting for the Update Time field in the Excel will also be according to your locale.

Updating Excel Template for Method 1

Figure 87: Adding Formatting for Excel Template

Figure 88: Generated Excel Using Method 1 After New Column Added

Changing Method 1 to Use Datapage

Although Method 1 has problem with the date/time formatting, it is able to take input from any type of pages, such as a Datapage.

Let us create a Datapage that retrieve the same data.

Since we are using a Datapage to generate the same list of operators, it is easier to specify the "*Object-type*" to be the same as that from the Report Definition, i.e. "*Data-Admin-Operator-ID*".

This will make the "*Response Data Transform*" field optional.

The following is the setting for the Datapage. Since the output is going to be a list, we need to change the "*Structure*" type to "*List*". We have also given a "*System name*" of "*FromRD*", which will remove a warning from the Guardrail.

Figure 89: Settings for D_GetListOfOperators

You can now run the Datapage, and you should get the following output:

Figure 90: Running Get List of Operators Via Datapage

Update DoExcelExport to Use Datapage

Figure 91: Adding D_GetListOfOperators to Pages & Classes

Note:
Since we are replacing the "pgRepPgSubSectionListUsersBBB", we can replace it with the D_GetListOfOperators instead; however, let us keep it there for reference purposes. In actual project implementation, it is always a best practice to remove unused pages from the "Pages & Classes".

Note:
Is it a best practice to specify the D_GetListOfOperators.pxResults type, even though it is not always mandatory.

Figure 92: Updated the Step Page as D_GetListOfOperators

Running with New D_GetListOfOperators

Fixing the Date Time Format

Update the New Field in the Template

Figure 93: Updated Template With Formatted Field Using pyNote

Note:
The value for the "Formatted Update Time" column is "{.pxResults().pyNote input}.

Upload the New Template

Figure 94: Upload The New Template With New pyNote Field

Figure 95: Upload File Confirmation Dialog

Modify the Datapage

Figure 96: Updated D_GetListOfOperators With Response Data Transform

Update the DoChangeListOfOperatorResponse DT

```
Primary -> Code-Pega-List
Primary.pxResults -> Data-Admin-Operator-ID
```

Figure 97: Pages & Classes for DoChangeListOfOperatorResponse DT

Figure 98: Adding A New Step 1 to Compute pyNote

```
Action:  "For Each Page"
Target:  ".pxResults"
Source:  Ticked
```

Step 1.1:

```
Action:  "Set"
Target:  ".pyNote"
Source:  "@FormatDateTime( .pxUpdateDateTime,
         "dd/MM/yyyy hh:mm:ss a",
         null, null)"
```

Save the rule.

Note:
You can keep the Step 2 above, it is meant for error handling, which we will ignore for now.

Note:
If you want to understand more about the different date/time formatting parameters, please refer to the "History" tab of the "FormatDateTime" function.

Testing the Formatted Date Time of Method 1

Figure 99: Generated Excel File With Formatted Update Time Column

Conclusion

In general, always try to use Method 2 first as it is easier and more maintainable. At the end of the day, users are mainly interested in data, and you should just provide it. Formatting, etc. should be done separately outside the Pega system for optimal efficiency, such as using Excel itself.

Method 1 is great for creating an actual Excel report, formatted accordingly to what you desired, as shown earlier. Another advantage of Method 1 is that you could also use Datapage as the source.

In terms of disadvantages, if the report is subjected to frequent changes, Method 1 would require more rules to be changed.

The other problem of Method 1 is with formatting. For example, if you need to have a DateTime field in the Excel, the default GMT format will be used, and you need to do extra work to format it.

Although, Method 2 can only be used with Report Definition, it is an easier way to export data to Excel.

If you have noticed, there is also a nice feature of Method 2, i.e. the columns comes with the "***Filter and Data***" feature, as shown below:

Figure 100: Method 2 Includes Filter and Data for All Columns

In terms of downside, Method 2 does not allow you to specify a filename for the downloaded Excel.

Apart from that, the Excel sheet tab is defaulted to "*Data*", and there is another additional tab, "*Info*". The values in this tab are also preconfigured and cannot be changed.

The following shows the additional tab.

Figure 101: Additional Tab Generated Using Method 2

Introducing Pega Snippets Series

Since there is already a "How-to" series, why create another Pega Snippets Series? The main reason is that writing a REAL book takes a lot of time and effort!

I have acquired a lot of knowledge and samples over the years, and if I were to share it via the traditional book publishing mechanism, it would take a long time to share all of those!

Therefore, a better way would be to share it via the Snippets Series, which is a collection of task-specific steps, with screenshots, to demonstrate how to do specific tasks in Pega.

What is the Main Difference Between Snippets and How-to Series?

The main focus of "Snippets" is on performing specific tasks in Pega, not on the 'why', other alternatives, or providing explanation of the potential problems that one might encountered. It also does not go into detailed explanation or discussion on the task/topic. In short, the focus is on accomplishing the task.

This means that in certain situations, and if you are not careful or not well-versed in Pega, the instructions might require some changes to make it work in your particular case.

On the other hand, the focus of the "How-to Guide", not only demonstrate the steps to accomplish the task, it also provides discussion, alternatives, and the "why" and "why-not".

In summary, "Snippets" would require more hand-on knowledge of Pega, which I believe, is a necessary trade-off.

How is Pega Snippets Distributed and the Price?

In general, Pega Snippets will be distributed as eBooks, for free.

The basis of Pega Snippets is to provide a quick sharing mechanism, which also mean that there would be a trade-off in terms of the details and content, as compared with the "How-to Guide" series.

Therefore, as far as the distribution platform supports, the 1st edition of every Pega Snippet shall be free. As more details and info are added to the Snippet, the price will increase.

Some platforms allow automatic updating of eBooks contents. This means that if you have added the Pega Snippet into your library, you will continue to get the updated content without further payment.

Example
The 1st Edition of a Pega Snippet was released in January, for free. Person A added it to his library at no cost.

In February, the Pega Snippet was updated, and the 2nd Edition was released for $1.99. Person B bought the 2nd Edition at $1.99.

In March, the Pega Snippet was again updated, and the 3rd Edition was released for $5.99. Person C bought the 3rd Edition at $5.99.

In the above example, Person A, B, C will all receive the same 3rd Edition of the Pega Snippet. However, it would cost Person C: $5.99, Person B: $1.99, and for Person A, it would still be free.

Given the above mechanism, it is always advisable to get the Pega Snippet as soon as it is released.

 Note: eBooks are published in colour. If you are using "Night/Dark Mode" on your device, images may appear as black/white.

Other Books in the Collections

Debunkum Beaver Pega CLSA Guide:
Preparing for Pega CLSA 7.3/7.4 Certification
(Book 1)

ISBN: 9789811703102
ISBN: 9781796641936

Debunkum Beaver Pega How-to Guide: Creating REST Service and REST Connector

ISBN: 9789811703171 (How-to Version)
ISBN: 9789811703188 (Master Beaver Version)

Debunkum Beaver Pega How-to Guide: Installing and Setting Up AES

ISBN: 9789811413599

Watch out for more releases at:
URL: https://www.DebunkumBeaver.com
Twitter: https://twitter.com/DebunkumBeaver

www.ingramcontent.com/pod-product-compliance
Lightning Source LLC
Chambersburg PA
CBHW070508090426
42735CB00012B/2698